without TRAFFIC:

EAST ANGLIA

John Brodribb

DIAL HOUSE

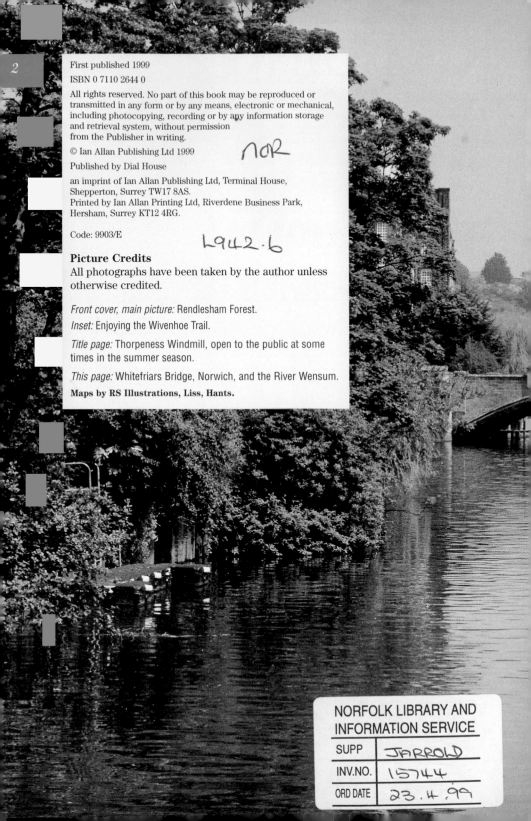

Published by Dial House

an imprint of Ian Allan Publishing Ltd, Terminal House,
Shepperton, Surrey TW17 8AS.
Printed by Ian Allan Printing Ltd, Riverdene Business Park,
Hersham, Surrey KT12 4RG.

Code: 9903/E

nor

L942.6

Picture Credits

All photographs have been taken by the author unless
otherwise credited.

Front cover, main picture: Rendlesham Forest.

Inset: Enjoying the Wivenhoe Trail.

Title page: Thorpeness Windmill, open to the public at some
times in the summer season.

This page: Whitefriars Bridge, Norwich, and the River Wensum.

Maps by RS Illustrations, Liss, Hants.

CONTENTS 🚲 *3*

HUNSTANTON

SHERINGHAM
CROMER
NORTH WALSHAM
FAKENHAM

⑤

④
② AYLSHAM
REEPHAM ③ STALHAM

⑥ KING'S LYNN

①

⑨ NORWICH

GREAT YARMOUTH

⑭

DOWNHAM MARKET

⑬ PETERBOROUGH

LOWESTOFT
㉓

BECCLES

THETFORD

⑦

SOUTHWOLD
⑧ ⑱
DUNWICH

㉒
SAXMUNDHAM
⑲ LEISTON
NEWMARKET DEBENHAM
⑫ ⑩ ALDEBURGH
CAMBRIDGE ⑰
⑪ WOODBRIDGE ⑯

㉗ ⑮ ㉑ IPSWICH
HADLEIGH
SUDBURY
NEWPORT ⑳ FELIXSTOWE
㉙ HARWICH
㉖ ㉚
㉕ ㉔ BRAINTREE COLCHESTER
BISHOP'S STORTFORD GT. DUNMOW

㉘

CHELMSFORD

East Anglia

Key

●   Town / City

① to ㉚   Routes

••••   NCN Hull - Harwich Route

ABOUT THIS BOOK

Cycling is one of the best ways to get out and enjoy the countryside. Travellers by car are isolated inside their vehicles and barely see the landscape rush by, whilst cyclists have the time to stop and stare if needs be. The same can be true of urban areas as well, although not everywhere is fully — or even partly — accessible to off-road cyclists.

There are great benefits to cycling. Cyclists are much healthier and so is the general environment in terms of lower energy usage, emissions of pollution and land-take. Wildlife is largely unaffected by cycling. The 'Safe Routes to School' initiative will allow far more children to walk and cycle to school, with great benefit

to the development of their social skills.

The aim of this book is to give some idea of where you can find off-road facilities in East Anglia. They are not entirely traffic-free, and the author feels it is important to indicate the possibilities in some of the larger towns of the region, where full implementation of the National Cycle Network should improve matters very greatly. Most of the routes are out in the country, and most are accessible by public transport. With increasing awareness of the need to carry bikes, train operators have made good progress with facilities on trains and at stations.

The landscape of East Anglia is very varied and visitors are usually surprised to find that it is not totally flat. These routes take you through the variety of scenery that the region has to offer. During the research in 1998 the weather was often dreadful, but much more importantly, the experience was great fun. Touring through the scenery and observing the wildlife was enjoyable and at times inspiring, and I hope that you enjoy using the book to get out and about in East Anglia. Some attractions along the routes are mentioned, but there are many more. Local Tourist Information Centres have full details and can help with accommodation. Note that most attractions make an admission charge, and that opening days and hours will vary. It is wise to check before visiting.

Left: Waymarkers for the Riverside and Railway Walks at Norwich. This marks the start of the route to Reepham and Aylsham, and is part of the NCN Hull to Harwich route.

Above: The Hunstanton line has been converted into an excellent cycle path within King's Lynn, and is seen here near the town centre. It is heavily used by local people, as well as being part of the Hull-Harwich route.

WHERE TO CYCLE

In many parts of Britain there are miles of disused railway lines and canal towpaths, both of which are increasingly being used for off-road cycling. East Anglia has neither in any quantity. The waterways system was based largely on rivers, the navigable portions of which penetrated only a relatively short distance inland. The Broads were one exception, but having been a by-product of peat extraction did not develop significant stretches of towpath. The boats used — keels and later wherries — were either sailed or quanted (a 'quant' is a long pole), although mechanical power arrived late in the day. In the Fens there were long stretches of drainage ditches, and many rivers were embanked and straightened for the same purpose. Again, navigation was often not the main purpose, although the wide strong banks may well find use as cycleways in the future.

It is therefore relatively difficult to find off-road routes, and there is a greater need to link them together by use of country lanes. To confound the matter further, a greater proportion of lanes were metalled than elsewhere: Suffolk has one of the highest in the country. Having obtained information from many sources, principally county and district councils, Forest Enterprises and Sustrans — to whom many thanks are due — as the basis of the routes in this book, the main types of route are described below.

Disused Railway Lines

East Anglia once had many more lines than today, and in spite of the low population density many places had duplicated facilities. The Great Eastern Railway had been the dominant company until near the end of the 19th century, only to find that the upstart Eastern & Midlands had designs on its territory. The traffic on offer was mainly agricultural, the holiday trade and fish. To cut a long story short, it was taken over by the Great Northern and Midland companies, becoming the celebrated Midland & Great Northern Joint. The programme of rail rationalisation, with the inevitable closures, began in earnest in the 1950s — long before Dr Beeching — and the Hadleigh branch lost its passenger services as long ago as 1932. For this reason, many did not survive long enough for their potential for alternative transport uses to be realised, and there are relatively few former lines used in this book.

Forestry Commission Land

In the guise of its commercial arm, Forest Enterprises, the Commission has made great strides in opening up its land for recreational use. Cycling is allowed on most hard tracks in the forest, and in many places routes are laid out and waymarked. Care must clearly be taken when using them, as forests are working environments where felling, extraction and other management may be in progress. The facilities provided within forests are often of a very high order, and they can be used as a day out on their own for people of all ages and abilities, or as staging points on longer cycle rides.

Rights of Way

There are many types, and the distinctions are important. Public footpaths are exactly what they say, and cannot be used by cyclists, although it may be possible to wheel a bike along some of them. Bridleways are also usable by horses and riders, and can be cycled: whether it is possible or practicable to do so is quite another matter. Byways open to all traffic (BOATs) and roads used as public paths (RUPPs) can also be cycled. Other routes are permissive, meaning that an activity is allowed but that there is no right to do so. It is possible, for example, to have a public footpath which is also a permissive cycle path.

Cycling is generally permitted on the public highway, although traffic levels and speeds understandably make many people nervous of so doing. Improvements are gradually being made, with the provision of measures such as cycle lanes, advance stop lines, contraflow lanes and so on. Cycling can be pleasant along the quieter C roads (yellow on Ordnance Survey maps), and along unclassified roads and tracks (yellow or white). In this book it has been

necessary to use the latter to link off-road sections, but this has been minimised and alternatives suggested where possible. In many instances it is possible to use these lanes to get from a railway station to the routes described.

THE NATIONAL CYCLE NETWORK

The National Cycle Network is being developed by Sustrans. It is a visionary project to provide an 8,000-mile network of cycle routes. Supported by a £43.5 million grant from the Millennium Commission, the network involves the active participation of more than 400 local authorities, the Department of the Environment, Transport and the Regions and other public and private bodies. It will provide a network of linked traffic-free paths, traffic-calmed and minor roads connecting urban centres and the countryside, and will reach all parts of the UK: 20 million people should be within two miles of it. It will provide a safe, attractive high-quality network for cyclists, as well as a major new amenity for walkers and wheelchair users. It is expected that 3,000 miles of millennium routes will be completed by 2000, and the remainder by 2005.

The principal section in East Anglia is the Hull to Harwich route, which will link King's Lynn with Fakenham, Norwich, Great Yarmouth, Lowestoft, Ipswich, Felixstowe, Colchester and Harwich. Although already signed on the ground for most of its route through the region, this is very much an interim stage, and much remains to be done to get more sections off-road. Other main routes run from the Lea Valley across through Harlow and Chelmsford to Colchester; north from Harlow through Cambridge, Ely and March; and from Ipswich through Bury St Edmunds to Cambridge and beyond. Yet another link goes north from Colchester through Bury and Thetford to Fakenham. These 'National' routes will be supplemented by large numbers of local networks, many of which are already in place as a result of local authority development.

PRACTICAL POINTS
Your Bike

Most of the routes in this book are suitable for any sort of bike: they are intended for pottering. The most popular type of machine these days is the mountain bike, which is more robust, has a better range of gears, wider, stronger tyres for better grip and can go almost anywhere. Bear in mind, however, that many off-road routes have barriers or gates of some sort to prevent access by motor bikes, so it may be necessary to lift your bike over these: lightness can be important. If in any doubt, try hiring, and when you find something that suits you, go to a specialist shop that is prepared to give you advice and help in choosing something suitable. Many hire centres in the more popular locations also have available machines including tandems, recumbents (where you lie back rather than sit up) and trailers for children.

Be sure that your bike is in good order when you get to the start of your trip. There are several points to check before leaving home:

• **Brakes** — check front and back to ensure that they are working, and also brake blocks and cables. Replace if worn.
• **Tyres** — check that they are fully pumped up. Check that tread is not worn or the valves damaged, otherwise the inner tube may need to be replaced.
• **Chain** — should be well-oiled and at the right tension.

• **Saddle** — check that it is at the right height. You should be able to pedal with your legs almost straight, but touch the ground with your toes when sitting in the saddle. This is especially important for children.
• **Gears** — check that they are working. Major adjustments probably need specialist attention.
• **Wheels** — check for broken spokes or buckled wheels. Specialist help may be needed here.
• **Lights** — check that they work front and back, and that you have spare batteries and bulbs.

- **Bell** — do have a bell fitted, and use it considerately. On cycle paths there are few things calculated to annoy other users more than a silent cyclist whooshing past suddenly.
- **Tool and puncture kits** — be sure to carry them! Practise mending punctures and changing tyres and inner tubes before you have to do it for real in the pouring rain of an English summer! A spare inner tube or two is a good idea. Your tool kit should contain at least: pump, Allen keys, adjustable spanner, screwdriver, at least two tyre levers and chain link remover. Don't hesitate to have your bike checked over by your local cycle repair shop before you set out, and also consider joining the Environmental Transport Association, which runs a breakdown service for motorists, but unlike the AA or RAC also offers a recovery service for cyclists.

Cycle Hire

Wherever practicable, the nearest cycle hire centre has been shown in the text. Many offer a variety of machines, but others have a more limited range and may need notice. It is always a good idea to contact them as far in advance as possible. It is often a good idea to travel to the location by public transport and then hire a bike, and it is certainly more environmentally friendly. Be sure that when you pick up the bike the hirer checks the frame size, adjusts the saddle and explains how the brakes and gears work. You should also get a tool kit.

Lock It Up!

It is an unfortunate fact that theft of bikes takes place even in rural areas, so security is important. Some rail stations now have secure stores, and there may also be racks, Sheffield stands and other means of securing them. Use a reinforced steel D-clamp if at all possible — others can be cut through much more easily. Keep a record of your frame number, and have it security postcoded.

Opposite page: A Sustrans information sign, near King's Lynn Sports Centre.

Below: Norwich is famous for its market, which provides a year-round splash of colour.

Above: Perhaps the best-known of the great museums in Cambridge is the Fitzwilliam.

Dressing the Part

You need to be comfortable and visible when cycling. Although the routes in the book are as traffic-free as possible, almost all of them involve crossing roads at the very least, and may necessitate cycling along them for short distances. Do try to wear something brightly coloured and reflective, especially in poor light.

Women will find it perfectly possible to cycle in a skirt, but do be sure that it won't get caught in the wheels. Divided skirts may be a better choice. Leggings or track suits which are tight at the leg are ideal: avoid anything too baggy which can be caught in the chain. Also avoid denim on longer rides, as it is relatively inflexible and has thick seams which can chafe. Consider padded cycling shorts if you are going to travel any distance — they can provide good protection against getting saddle-sore. You may also find that gloves are useful, especially when the weather is cold. Your hands are very exposed, even when the rest of you is warm.

For the upper body it is best to have several thinner layers rather than one thick one: it is easier to adjust your temperature as the day or your body warms up. A fleece provides an excellent outer garment, and can have very few or many layers underneath, depending on the season. Don't forget to carry cream for protection against sunburn, especially if you have children. Cycling along in bright sunshine in a breeze, it can be very easy to overlook the effects of the sun.

Be aware also that the weather can change very quickly. You may set out under a fine clear blue sky, but it can quickly become cold and showery. Carry a kagoule at the least, and consider also waterproof trousers; the research for this book was done mostly in the exceptionally wet summer of 1998 — they help a great deal!

Almost any flat-soled footwear will do for cycling — trainers are ideal. Do make sure that laces are tied properly so that they do not tangle in anything.

Helmets

There continues to be debate about the need for cycle helmets. Children are increasingly wearing them, but many adults still feel that they are uncomfortable. What is not in question is that they can prevent or reduce head injuries resulting from accidents where a cyclist is thrown to the ground. The resulting disabilities include personality changes, prolonged coma or inability to concentrate. The brain may be penetrated by fragments of bone, or may suffer pressure damage.

According to the Bicycle Helmet Initiative Trust and Headway, approximately 100,000 young people are injured annually through bicycle accidents, and account for half of all cycling casualties. The British Association of Insurers estimates the annual cost to the nation is in excess of £1,000 million. Brain injury is the single major cause (70%) of death and disability of children, and cycle helmets are proven to be effective in reducing head injuries in young people by 85%.

Helmets need to fit well and be comfortable. Hearing and vision must not be impaired by wearing. They should be ventilated so that a cooling flow of air is provided, especially to the forehead, and style is important, not least for children. Try before you buy! Cycle hirers should also have them available.

It is important to remember that a helmet will not prevent an accident: the wearer is not invulnerable. The majority of accidents are caused by motorists at or near junctions, so defensive riding is essential. Helmets are not yet compulsory, but the only possible advice is to wear one at all times.

Children

Almost all the rides in the book are suitable for children, although those in the urban areas usually involve going on to roads. It may be preferable to find safe parking for your bike and take the bus or train into the town centre. Where you have young children, the easier rides may be preferable: stop for frequent breaks as they can tire easily and become fractious. Carry refreshments for them. Take care where crossing roads and on seemingly quiet lanes where some car drivers delight in speeding excessively. Do set a good example with your own behaviour, such as wearing a helmet.

Refreshments

Potential stopping places have been indicated wherever possible, but there are many others. Do carry drinks and at least some food — snack bars or fruit — since you will not always be near a shop or tea room.

Checklist

You may find this list useful:
• cycle repair kit, including spare inner tube(s)
• pump
• waterproofs
• water bottle(s)

- suntan cream
- insect repellent (especially for forest routes)
- food of some sort
- lock
- money
- clean rag or hand wipes
- lights
- reflective belt or clothing
- maps and guide books
- hat and gloves

These various items can be carried in a pannier or pair of panniers strapped to a carrier at the rear of your bike. Some have a carrier which allows a rucksack to be securely strapped to it, whilst others may have a front basket. Don't carry things on your back — it will unbalance you, and make you sweaty. Don't have any loose or trailing straps.

Below: Bridleway near Earl Soham, on the way to Bedfield and Tannington.

TRANSPORTING YOUR BIKE

The bike is a sustainable, environmentally friendly form of transport. It creates almost no pollution and uses only the energy from your food. The ideal situation is therefore to arrive at your destination by bike, or having come by bus or rail. You can then hire a bike, or bring your own on the train. There will be situations, of course, where the use of a car is a necessity, and there are now many types of carrier available.

Carrying by Car

The back carrier fits to the car by straps, clips and adjustable angles, and can usually carry two bikes. More expensive carriers fit onto the tow bar and can hold up to four bikes: neither must obscure the number plate or lights. Care is also needed not to damage car or bike paintwork.

Roof racks are another possibility, either holding the bikes right way up or upside down. Although vision is not obstructed, considerable strength is needed to get bikes up there without damage. Large estate cars and people carriers can be used, but this may restrict the number of passengers. Quick-release wheels will mean that bikes will fit into most cars. Carry an old blanket to prevent damage to the car or other bikes, and to protect from mud at the end of a ride. Remove accessories before you fix your bike on or in the car. Always lock your bike rack inside your car while you are away from it, and if you are leaving bikes unattended on it for any length of time, lock them to each other and the car.

Public Transport

In East Anglia this means trains. Buses can get you to the start of a route and a cycle hire centre, but there are not yet bike-carrying buses in the area. With the present structure of the rail industry, each operator has a different policy on carriage of bikes, although there is an increasing provision for storage at stations. The train operators in East Anglia are:
• **Anglia Railways** — InterCity services from London Liverpool Street to Norwich and Harwich International; local services in Norfolk and Suffolk. Space can be reserved and is officially recommended: up to four bikes on local trains (six on InterCity) using specially modified units, otherwise, first-come, first-served. £1 flat fare, accompanying whatever passenger ticket you have, on all local trains, and InterCity trains between Norwich and Colchester. Anglia also now operates a free cycle rescue service through the Environmental Transport Association: see leaflets for details. No tandems on local trains. No bikes on trains between Norwich and Yarmouth on Saturdays in July and August between 09.00 and 13.00. Note that the InterCity service on the Norwich main line will have many new three-car trains introduced in May 1999, which will have the cycle carrying capacity of the local trains only.
• **Central Trains** — services from the Midlands and northwest to Norwich, Cambridge and Stansted Airport. Reservations are required; up to two bikes per train. Flat fee of £3 per single journey or day return.
• **Great Eastern Railway** — services from London Liverpool Street to Southend Victoria, Southminster, Ipswich, Clacton, Walton, Harwich, Braintree and the Sudbury branch. Carried free. Not permitted on trains arriving in London between 07.45 and 09.45, or leaving between 16.30 and 18.30. On slam-door trains, must be carried with the conductor.
• **Great North Eastern Railway** — fast trains on the East Coast main line serving Peterborough. £3 charge, reservations required.
• **West Anglia Great Northern** — services from London Liverpool Street to Cambridge and Ely; also London King's Cross to Stansted Airport, Cambridge, Ely, King's Lynn and Peterborough. Carried free. Not permitted on trains arriving in London before 09.30 Mondays to Fridays (except bank holidays), or leaving London between 16.00 and 19.00. Tandems and three-wheelers are not permitted.

In general, cyclists should remain near their bikes. Journeys between operators are usually charged at £3 per bike per single journey. Where bus substitutions are made, for example where engineering work is taking place, bikes cannot be carried on the replacement buses. Many stations now have lockers and stands available for cycle storage.

Opposite page:
On the Flitch Way near Great Dunmow.

Right: The junction of the Valley Walk and Stour Valley path, about 1½ miles from Sudbury station.

Below: Debenham is an old and interesting town, with many interesting buildings.

ROUTE 1

MARRIOTT'S WAY — NORWICH TO REEPHAM

PLACES OF INTEREST ALONG THE ROUTE

The Marriott's Way is named after William Marriott, once Chief Engineer and Manager of the Midland & Great Northern Joint Railway. It follows the course of two lines, one the M&GN route from Norwich City to Melton Constable, and the other the Great Eastern line from Wroxham to County School. The two crossed at Themelthorpe, and when the M&GN closed to passengers, the journey for goods traffic between Norwich Thorpe and City stations was some 60 miles via Sheringham. The Themelthorpe curve was built, halving this. After both lines closed completely most of

Starting point: An easy ride. Strictly speaking, the Marriott's Way starts at Hellesdon Road in New Costessey. However, it is continuous with the Norwich Riverside Path, and the two are considered together here. The route is described from the roundabout on St Crispins Road (see Route 9).

Parking: Hellesdon Road; Costessey Lane, Drayton; Freeland Corner near Felthorpe; Attlebridge station (note that the station itself is private property); Lenwade station; Whitwell Community Woodland (at Whitwell & Reepham old station).

Public transport: Anglia Railways and Central Trains to Norwich. Frequent buses from Norwich to Hellesdon, Costessey and Drayton, infrequent to Attlebridge, Lenwade and Reepham.

Cycle hire: Anglia Bike Centre, 72a Gloucester Street, Norwich (01603 632467); Freewheel, 75 Prince of Wales Road, Norwich NR1 1DG (01603 610072);

the route became a permissive cycle, horse and footpath. The section from Reepham to Aylsham is covered by Route 2.

Reepham station is home to cycle hire (summer only) and an excellent tea room and gift shop. Foxley Wood is a Norfolk Wildlife Trust site, open all year, and with free access. It is noted for its wildflowers, butterflies and birds, especially woodpeckers (01603 625540). The Norfolk Wildlife Park at Great Witchingham is best reached from the Blackwater access point, along minor lanes. It is open daily from April to October (01603 872274). The Dinosaur Adventure Park is on the other side of the A1067 near Lenwade and is open April to September (01603 870245). For details of Norwich, see Route 9.

Reepham station, Reepham, NR10 4LJ (01603 871187).

Distance: About 15 miles one way from Norwich to Reepham taking the shortcut; about 19 miles via Themelthorpe.

Maps: OS Landranger 133 (North East Norfolk); Reepham station leaflet; Marriott's Way leaflet (both leaflets from Tourist Information Centres). Sustrans Fakenham to Harwich, panels 1 and 2.

Surfaces and gradients: No significant gradients. Surfaces are generally good but may be soft: the route is shared with horses and can be muddy in places. See the notes about the Themelthorpe link path.

Roads and crossing points: Off-road all the way. There are a few level crossings of minor roads where the railway once crossed; the A1067 is crossed at Drayton, and also the B1145 if using the Themelthorpe link.

National Cycle Network connections: Norwich-Reepham-Themelthorpe is part of the Hull to Harwich route.

Refreshments: Reepham has some excellent pubs, tea rooms and shops. Reepham station. Foulsham (about a mile

west of Themelthorpe) has shops and a pub. Norwich has all facilities.

ROUTE INSTRUCTIONS

Not necessary. Start at the St Crispins Road Roundabout (or any of the car parks mentioned) and follow the signs.

You have a choice when you get to the old Whitwell & Reepham station. You can:

1. Either take the short cut to the town. Turn right at the end of the platforms, along the station approach and onto the main road (take care). Turn left and right immediately before the bridge, along a bridleway (it is possible to reach this from a steep muddy track down from the railway trackbed just after the bridge, but don't try

Opposite page: Marriott's Way marker.

Below: The start of the Railway Path at Norwich. This is more or less the site of the old Norwich City station, now partly covered by a road. The first part of the route has been metalled.

to ride down it). Continue along a field headland, coming to a T-junction. The official short cut goes left, but having crossed the B1145 (take care — go right then left) the surface deteriorates badly. Instead turn right (the path is called Broomhill Lane) emerging past the High School and turn left into the town.

2. Or continue on the railway trackbed via Themelthorpe, coming out at Reepham station.

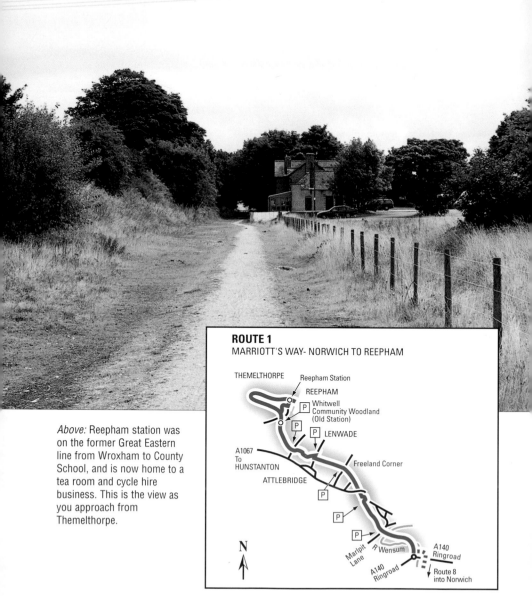

Above: Reepham station was on the former Great Eastern line from Wroxham to County School, and is now home to a tea room and cycle hire business. This is the view as you approach from Themelthorpe.

ROUTE 1
MARRIOTT'S WAY- NORWICH TO REEPHAM

THEMELTHORPE   Reepham Station
REEPHAM
P Whitwell
   Community Woodland
   (Old Station)
P
P LENWADE
A1067
To
HUNSTANTON   Freeland Corner
ATTLEBRIDGE
P
P
P
Marlpit   R Wensum   A140
Lane   Ringroad
      A140   Route 8
      Ringroad   into Norwich
N

MARRIOTT'S WAY — REEPHAM TO AYLSHAM

PLACES OF INTEREST ALONG THE ROUTE

Reepham station: see Route 1. Blickling Hall (National Trust) is an imposing Jacobean structure with extensive grounds including ornamental lakes, gardens, an orangery and picnic area. The ride links with Routes 1 (to Norwich) and 4 (Aylsham to North Walsham). Aylsham is home to the Bure Valley Railway, which operates from May to September (not Fridays and Saturdays in May, June and September), and at some other times (01263 733858). Bikes can be carried for £2 (1998 fare).

Left: Cycling along the Marriott's Way near Cawston.

infrequent to Cawston and Reepham.

Cycle hire: Anglia Bike Centre, 72a Gloucester Street, Norwich (01603 632467); Freewheel, 75 Prince of Wales Road, Norwich NR1 1DG: (01603 610072); Reepham station, Reepham, NR10 4LJ (01603 871187); Stoners, 35 Red Lion Street, Aylsham (01263 733252).

Distance: About 6½ miles one way from Reepham to Aylsham. The link to the Weavers' Way, avoiding Aylsham, is about 1½ miles and also gives off-road access (poor surface) to Blickling Hall.

Starting point: Reepham station. An easy ride.

Parking: Whitwell Community Woodland (at Whitwell & Reepham old station); Reepham station (as with so many places, Reepham once had two railway stations!); Bure Valley station, Aylsham.

Public transport: Anglia Railways to Wroxham; Bure Valley Railway from Wroxham to Aylsham (seasonal, 01263 733858). Frequent buses from Norwich, Cromer and Sheringham to Aylsham;

Maps: OS Landranger 133 (Northeast Norfolk); Reepham station leaflet; Marriott's Way leaflet (both leaflets from Tourist Information Centres). Sustrans Fakenham to Harwich, panel 1.

Surfaces and gradients: No significant gradients, except at Cawston where the path has to avoid the privately owned station. Surfaces are generally good but may be soft: the route is shared with horses and can be muddy in places.

Roads and crossing points: Off-road all the way. There are a few level crossings of minor roads where the railway once crossed. At the Aylsham end, the Bure Valley station is on the other side of the busy B1354.

National Cycle Network connections: Reepham-Themelthorpe is part of the Hull to Harwich route.

Refreshments: Reepham has some excellent pubs, tea rooms and shops. Refreshments at Reepham station. Cawston has the Bell pub and shops. Aylsham has several pubs, a tea room and a range of shops. The Bure Valley Railway station has a café and also a seasonal Tourist Information Centre. Tea rooms at Blickling Hall.

ROUTE INSTRUCTIONS
Not necessary. Start at Reepham station and follow the signs. The link to the Weavers' Way and Blickling Hall is a left turn about a mile short of Aylsham station and is clearly signed. See also Route 4.

Below: Parts of the Marriott's Way have been divided between horse riders and pedestrians/cyclists. This shows one of the markers near Reepham.

Opposite: There were very many level crossings on both railway routes that make up the Marriott's Way, and present-day users also have to cross the same lanes. This is a typical gateway, near Aylsham.

ROUTE 2
MARRIOTT'S WAY- REEPHAM TO AYLSHAM

To Blickling Hall
and Weavers Way
(Route 3)

AYLSHAM

P

Aylsham Station
(Bure Valley Railway)

To A140
Norwich

THEMELTHORPE

P Reepham
Station

CAWSTON

REEPHAM

P Whitwell
Community Woodland
(Old Station)

To Norwich
(Route 1)

N

MARRIOTT'S WAY

This former railway line is not a public right of way.
Residents and Visitors to Norfolk are permitted to use it
at their own risk as a footpath, cycleway and bridleway.

Please respect wildlife, keep dogs under control and
take your litter home.

No vehicular access. No shooting. No camping.

NORFOLK COUNTY COUNCIL

WEAVERS' WAY — STALHAM TO BENGATE

PLACES OF INTEREST ALONG THE ROUTE

Stalham is on the Norfolk Broads, and has boatyards and can offer trips out. The North Walsham & Dilham Canal was one of the less successful navigations. It was made by improving the River Ant, but hampered by lack of water. It can be walked from Tonnage Bridge, recently restored, to Honing Lock, and is fascinating for students of industrial archaeology. Sutton Windmill is about 2 miles east of Stalham, also on the Weavers' Way, and is Britain's tallest. Its corn-milling machinery is complete and it also has fine museum displays of bygone domestic life, together with local rural trades.

North Walsham is an interesting small town, noted for its Market Cross. The Norfolk Motor Cycle Museum is in the station yard, Norwich Road (01692 406266).

Starting point(s): An easy ride. Stalham (old railway station), Bengate.

Parking: Bengate, opposite side of road (A149) from the Weavers' Way; Stalham.

Public transport: Anglia Railways to North Walsham: it would be relatively easy to start from here and use quiet lanes to link with the route. Worstead station is also nearby. First Eastern Counties bus services to North Walsham, and infrequently to Stalham.

Cycle hire: Sutton Staithe boatyard (01692 581653); Bike Riders, North Walsham (01692 406632).

Distance: About 5 miles each way; a further 3 miles into North Walsham.

Left: The Weavers' Way is a long-distance path from Great Yarmouth to Cromer, with two sections along old railway lines. This part is near Stalham.

Maps: OS Landranger 133 (North East Norfolk); Explorer 25 (Norfolk Coast East).

Surfaces and gradients: Surfaces are mostly compacted ballast, generally good but occasionally stony. No significant gradients, except at Bengate where the path goes from the top of the embankment down to road level.

Roads and crossing points: A minor lane near Stalham, and two near Honing. The route into North Walsham is along minor lanes, with the exception of a short stretch along the Happisburgh (pronounced 'Haysboro') Road.

National Cycle Network connections: Norwich is the nearest point. It is possible (having negotiated North Walsham) to ride off-road almost all the way from Stalham to Aylsham (see Route 4) and then to Norwich via the Marriott's Way (see Routes 1 and 2).

Refreshments: Stalham and North Walsham have all facilities. The Butchers Arms at East Ruston is about ¾-mile off the route.

ROUTE INSTRUCTIONS

The route is along the part of the old Midland & Great Northern railway line between Great Yarmouth and Melton Constable. This section starts at Stalham station, still intact but in use as a Norfolk County Council highways depot. Beware of the signed cycle route by the main road: instead go through the gate onto the Weavers' Way.

Above: The Weavers' Way reaches North Walsham via country lanes, and there is much of interest on the way. This is the Baptist Church at Worstead. The woollen cloth of that name originated in the village.

Further instructions are unnecessary unless you wish to continue into North Walsham. Follow the Weavers' Way except where this crosses fields by means of footpaths. At Bengate, turn right along the lane. Continue along this lane and through the next hamlet where you will pick up Weavers' Way signs. Follow these into North Walsham. Note that the right turn across the field, from Field Lane, (having turned left off the Happisburgh Road) is a footpath, but is heavily cycled. It is possible to follow Weavers' Way signs through the town centre and link with Route 4, but they will take you against the direction of the one-way system, so it is necessary to wheel bikes.

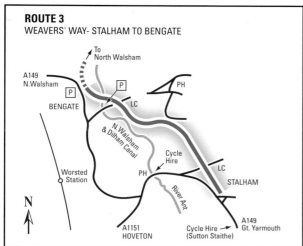

ROUTE 3
WEAVERS' WAY- STALHAM TO BENGATE

To North Walsham
A149 N.Walsham
P
P
PH
BENGATE
LC
N. Walsham & Dilham Canal
Cycle Hire
LC
Worsted Station
PH
STALHAM
River Ant
N
A1151 HOVETON
Cycle Hire (Sutton Staithe)
A149 Gt. Yarmouth

Above: Only the platforms remain at Honing station, although there is now a picnic site there. The original bridge over the North Walsham & Dilham canal (the canalised River Ant) has long gone, replaced with this one.

WEAVERS' WAY — NORTH WALSHAM TO AYLSHAM

PLACES OF INTEREST ALONG THE ROUTE

See also Route 2. Aylsham is an interesting market town with book and antique shops. It is home to the Bure Valley Railway, a narrow-gauge line built on the trackbed of the former Great Eastern line from Wroxham. It operates from May to September (not Fridays and Saturdays in May, June and September), and at other times (01263 733858). Blickling Hall (National Trust) is an imposing Jacobean structure with extensive grounds including ornamental lakes, gardens, an orangery and picnic area.

Starting point(s): Easy ride. North Walsham; Aylsham.

Parking: North Walsham (from the Yarmouth direction, turn left off the A149, under the railway bridge and right almost immediately; the Weavers' Way car park is about ¼-mile on the left); Felmingham old railway station and butterfly reserve; Aylsham's Weavers' Way car park is at the old North station, opposite an industrial estate. From the Norwich direction, go past the town on the A140, and turn left about 1¾ miles after the roundabout; the car park is about ½-mile along this road.

Public transport: Anglia Railways' trains to North Walsham. Frequent First Eastern Counties bus services between Norwich and Cromer. Bure Valley trains from Hoveton & Wroxham (£2 charge for bikes — 1998 fare), which connect with Anglia Railways.

Cycle hire: Bike Riders, North Walsham (01692 406632); Stoners, Aylsham (01263 733252).

Below: A Weavers' Way sign on a gate.

Distance: About six miles each way. Links with Routes 1 and 2.

Maps: OS Landranger 133 (Northeast Norfolk); Explorer 25 (Norfolk Coast East).

Surfaces and gradients: No significant gradients. Surfaces are usually compacted ballast, although at the Aylsham end there are some rough tracks where the route leaves the old railway line. If linking off-road with the Marriott's Way, there is a short section on rough grass.

Roads and crossing points: Having got on to the route at North Walsham, nothing until crossing the A140 north of Aylsham; B1354 to Blickling just north of Aylsham.

National Cycle Network connections: See Route 2.

Refreshments: North Walsham and Aylsham have all facilities. There is a café at Aylsham station, on the Bure Valley Railway. Tea rooms at Blickling Hall.

ROUTE INSTRUCTIONS

From North Walsham station go down to the road, turn left and then right almost at once. Follow this road until you come to the Weavers' Way on your left. From town centre, pick up Weavers' Way signs (not easy) by the Aylsham Road railway bridge, which will lead you onto the trackbed of the former Midland & Great Northern line. Beware: the signs will take you against the flow of traffic in the one-way system.

No further instructions needed until you reach Aylsham. The Weavers' Way leaves the trackbed just before reaching the A140, but is clearly signed. It is easy to make your way into the town from a number of points. If you wish to access the Marriott's Way without going into Aylsham, follow the signs until you cross the B1354 (take care). The route climbs steeply out of the old railway cutting: turn left onto the old road (right for an off-road link to Blickling Hall), and follow the path to where it turns right onto a wide grassy tree-lined avenue. Almost at the end of this there is a gate in the fence on the left: go through this, along

Below: The Weavers' Way railway path to Aylsham starts near the centre of North Walsham. The former trackbed drops down here to pass under the still-used Great Eastern line to Cromer.

the track to the road and turn left. Take the first right (a track), past Manor Farm, and don't turn off it — it becomes Green Lane and leads to the Marriott's Way about a mile west of Aylsham station.

Below: At Felmingham station the cutting has been developed as a butterfly reserve and the banks of the cutting are rich in the wildflowers and bushes that are their food plants. Information boards are provided; users are asked not to stray from the main track.

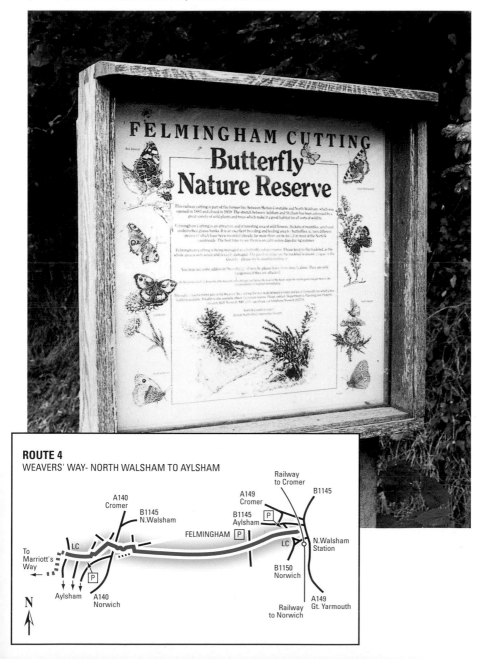

ROUTE 4
WEAVERS' WAY- NORTH WALSHAM TO AYLSHAM

PEDDARS' WAY — FRING TO GREAT MASSINGHAM

PLACES OF INTEREST ALONG THE ROUTE

Bircham windmill has been fully restored to working order, and is open daily: you can buy your bread there. Sandringham is well-known as a royal retreat, and house and grounds (Tel: 01553 772675) are usually open to the public between April and October. Castle Acre is a historic village with a ruined priory and castle (English Heritage, Tel: 01760 755394). It is actually on the Peddars Way, reached along a fairly busy metalled section about five miles south of the end of this route. Beware of trying to park there. Houghton Hall (Tel: 01485 528569), seat of the Marquess of Cholmondeley, is one of the grandest surviving Palladian houses in England. The house, model soldier museum, park and garden are open Sundays, Thursdays and Bank Holidays from Easter to the end of September.

Starting point: Bircham Windmill.

Parking: Bircham Windmill, Great Massingham village, B1153 where it crosses the Peddars Way, Harpley Dams (south of A148).

Public transport: The nearest rail connection is King's Lynn. Frequent buses from King's Lynn bus station to Heacham, about a mile from Sedgeford.

Cycle hire: Bircham windmill (Tel: 01485 578393).

Distance: About 14 miles one way; short cuts possible.

Maps: OS Landranger 132 (Northwest Norfolk); Explorer 23 (Norfolk Coast West).

Surfaces and gradients: A relatively easy

Below: The restored windmill at Bircham, which is open daily. It is very convenient for the Peddars Way.

ride; mostly hard country track, some sections grassy; gently undulating.

Roads and crossing points: Short section on very minor lanes at the windmill and at Fring; three minor lanes crossed near Fring; B1153, A148 at Harpley Dams; three lanes and B1145 near Great Massingham.

National Cycle Network connections: The Hull to Harwich route passes through King's Lynn and Sedgeford, the latter under a mile from Fring.

Refreshments: Bircham windmill has an excellent tea-room, open daily from Easter to September; pubs and shops at Harpley, Anmer, Castle Acre and Great Massingham; shop, hotel and restaurant at Great Bircham; tea-room at Houghton Hall (when open).

ROUTE INSTRUCTIONS
From Bircham windmill there are several options at the start:
• Turn left from the car park, right at the end of the lane, and left after about a mile onto an excellent but unsigned track. Go left onto the Peddars Way after about ½mile.
• or turn right from the car park, and follow the lane in a northerly direction to Fring (about 2 miles). Turn left then right almost at once, and after a further mile, turn left onto the Peddars Way.

Right: An interesting collection of waymarks on the Peddars Way, near Great Massingham.

• or turn right from the car park, follow the lane in a northerly direction for about ¾-mile, turning right onto a grassy track. After ½-mile take an acute left turn, and follow this track to Fring, turning left at the road. Continue along this to the Peddars Way, or take the first (or second right). This is the longest option.

• or turn right from the car park, follow the lane in a northerly direction for nearly a mile and turn left at the pump house. Just over a mile, and a crossing of a lane brings you to the Peddars Way.

Continue along the Peddars Way: being a Roman Road, it is fairly straight! Take care crossing the A148. Turning left at any of the next four lanes will take you to Great Massingham. At the one after that the Peddars Way becomes a moderately busy metalled road, and leads to Castle Acre after about 5 miles.

ROUTE 5
PEDDARS WAY- FRING TO GREAT MASSINGHAM

FRING

Bircham Windmill (cycle hire)

GREAT BIRCHAM

B1153

ANMER

HARPLEY

Harpley Dams

A148

GREAT MASSINGHAM

N

B1145

To Castle Acre

Above: The Peddars Way near Anmer. This Roman road ended at Holme, on the north Norfolk coast, and can be cycled for much of its length.

KING'S LYNN

PLACES OF INTEREST ALONG THE ROUTE

King's Lynn has numerous attractions, and many buildings in the docks areas have been well restored. Located in Saturday Market Place is the Guildhall and Tourist Information Centre (01553 763044) and the Old Gaol House. The latter has interactive displays and stories of infamous murderers, highwaymen and witches. The Town House Museum of Lynn Life (01553 773450) is adjacent in Queen Street. Nearby is Purfleet Quay and the Custom House. Queen Street and King Street are lined by many fine buildings, the latter having the splendid Guildhall of St George. There is also much of the old town in evidence, and much of the centre is pedestrianised. The Lynn Museum (01553 775001) is near the bus station. True's Yard museum (01553 770479) tells the story of King's Lynn's old fishing community.

Starting point: Rail station, or NCN Route 1, either approaching from the north or west.

Parking: Multi-storey car park next to the bus station.

Public transport: West Anglia Great Northern trains from London, Cambridge and Ely; buses from many parts of Norfolk.

Cycle hire: Fat Birds Don't Fly, 22 Greevegate, Hunstanton (01485 535875); Bircham Windmill (01485 578393); A. E. Wallis, 36 High Street, Heacham (01485 571683).

Maps: OS Landranger 132 (Northwest Norfolk), Explorer 23 (Norfolk Coast West); Sustrans Hull to Fakenham, panel 3; Norfolk Coast by Bike leaflet (£2) from Tourist Information Centres; King's Lynn mini-guide (free).

Surfaces and gradients: Mostly metalled. No significant gradients.

Below: King's Lynn is a port on the Wash, where the River Great Ouse flows to the sea. NCN Route 1 passes through the town, and is seen here approaching from the south and west along the river.

Above: There is much history in King's Lynn: on the cycle approach from the south is Whitefriars Gate, once entrance to a Carmelite friary occupied from 1260 to 1538. Here Friar Aleyn wrote *The Book of Margery Kempe*, earliest known biography in the English language, circa 1436-40.

Roads and crossing points: Much of the centre of King's Lynn is traffic-free, but not all can be cycled. The main route through the town is largely off-road.

National Cycle Network connections: King's Lynn is on the Hull to Harwich route.

Refreshments: The town has all facilities.

ROUTE INSTRUCTIONS
The NCN Hull to Harwich route provides the main cycleway through the town. It is possible to follow the signed NCN Route 1 to or from Wiggenhall St Germans (see Route 14). In Lynn, a pedestrian shared-use cycle path follows the east bank of the Great Ouse river from the Free Bridge (the NCN joins a little further along, from St Valery Lane) and then across the River Nar, passing Whitefriars Gate. Follow signs to the town centre, bus station and railway station, but beware of the one-way system and the need to dismount in pedestrian areas.

If arriving by train, turn left from the forecourt onto a pedestrian shared-use path. To go westward and to the town centre follow round to the right. To go north and east (Hunstanton and Norwich) turn left at the T-junction, coming out near a railway level crossing. Cross the road by traffic lights, over the railway and turn right onto the path, signed to Sandringham. This quickly picks up the trackbed of the former railway to Hunstanton and follows it for about ½-mile to the crossing of the A148 (take care), and on to the A1078 crossing (take care). The former railway line in King's Lynn is part of the National Cycle Network.

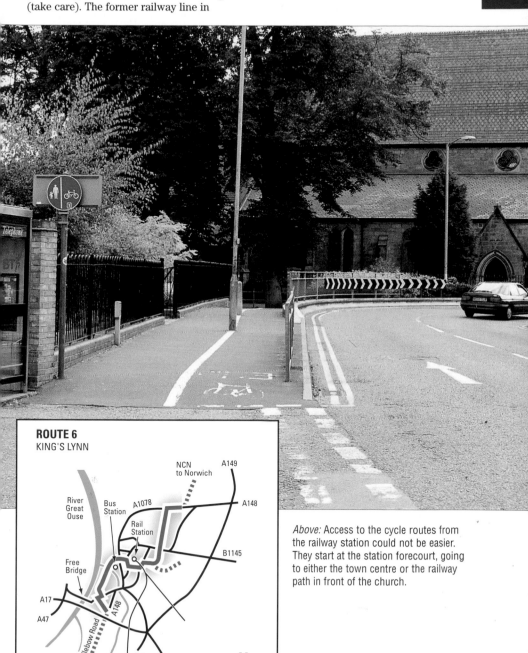

ROUTE 6
KING'S LYNN

Above: Access to the cycle routes from the railway station could not be easier. They start at the station forecourt, going to either the town centre or the railway path in front of the church.

THETFORD FOREST PARK

PLACES OF INTEREST ALONG THE ROUTE

Brandon is an interesting small town, once a major centre for the flint industry. The Heritage Centre in George Street (open Easter to October) includes a flint-knapper's workshop and relives the town's history from Neolithic times to the present day. If you follow the High Lodge circuit, there are open-air reminders and information displays about the flint industry.

The best-known centre for flint mining is at Grimes Graves, which can be reached from the A1065 about 4 miles northeast of Brandon. The site is owned by English Heritage and is open daily from April to October.

If you follow the Brandon Park loop, watch out for information boards about birds in the forest, especially crossbills. There is a public hide just off the route.

Starting point(s): Brandon Country Park Visitor Centre or High Lodge Forest Centre. Note that there is a per-car charge for entry to High Lodge.

Parking: As above; also Mayday Farm off B1106 between Brandon and Elveden.

Public transport: Central Trains services to Brandon, about 1½ miles from the route.

Cycle hire: At High Lodge (01842 815078 day, 0589 100831 [mobile] after 6pm).

Distance: Two circuits of 6½ miles each.

Below. The link between the two loops at Thetford also has car parking available at Mayday Farm. Signing is very good throughout the forest.

Opposite: Look out for this carving at High Lodge!

ROUTE 7
THETFORD FOREST PARK

Maps: OS Landranger 144 (Thetford & Breckland); Cycling in the Forest: Thetford Forest Park leaflet, from Forest Enterprises offices.

Surfaces and gradients: Easy rides. Forest tracks, generally well-drained, possibly sandy, possibly muddy in places. Gradients are mostly gentle, but not always. The High Lodge circuit is the easier of the two, but is much busier.

Roads and crossing points: If starting from Brandon station, the initial section is along the busy A1065 between the station and town centre; part of the town is traffic-free, but there is a further ¾-mile on the B1106 before reaching the turning for Brandon Country Park. Path between the two circuits (about ½-mile) crosses the B1106.

National Cycle Network connections: The route between Ipswich and Cambridge passes through Bury St Edmunds (about 15 miles from Brandon) which itself has a number of cycle routes.

Refreshments: Brandon Country Park Visitor Centre sells drinks, sandwiches and snacks; High Lodge Forest Centre has a café and other refreshments; Brandon has all facilities, including an excellent fish and chip restaurant.

ROUTE INSTRUCTIONS

These are hardly necessary, especially if you have the leaflet. From Brandon, the Country Park is about ¾-mile along the Bury Road (B1106) on the right. Follow the waymarks from the Visitor Centre: at the first intersection, go right. Later you will be offered a choice of long and short routes: only the long route lets you link with the High Lodge circuit.

When approaching the B1106, near Mayday Farm, there is clear signing either back to the Centre or to High Lodge.

If starting from High Lodge, note that there is no cycling within the recreation area. The cycle path skirts the edge and has access to the bike hire facility. The route is clearly waymarked. Look out for the totem pole! As with all Forest Enterprise rides, do keep a lookout for signs of forestry activity, and heed any signs and diversions.

Below: Few places can be better for gentle recreational cycling than Thetford Forest. There is plenty of shelter, the surfaces are good, with refreshments and toilets available at Brandon Country Park and High Lodge, with cycle hire at the latter.

ICKNIELD WAY — EUSTON TO KENNETT

PLACES OF INTEREST ALONG THE ROUTE

Thetford is a town where the old and new coexist uneasily. It has many flint-walled buildings as befits its Breckland position, but it has also been much expanded in recent years, with new housing, industry and the inevitable big roads. In the centre is a fine statue of Thomas Paine, author of the Rights of Man. The town's history is long, and it boasts the Ancient House museum (01842 752599), priory ruins (there were three priories), the castle earthworks and from the more recent industrial past, the Charles Burrell museum. Knettishall Heath and West Stow have country parks; more details of Thetford Forest and its facilities are given under Route 7.

Lackford, southeast of Icklingham, is a major reserve based on sand and gravel pits, and is managed by the Suffolk Wildlife Trust (01473 890089) for its bird life. Cavenham Heath is a national nature reserve managed by English Nature, part of which has unrestricted access. Newmarket is covered under Route 10.

Starting point(s): A fairly easy ride. Knettishall Heath, Euston, Thetford Heath (next to the Air Products depot).

Parking: Euston; byway immediately to the west of the Air Products depot (turn off to Elveden at the traffic lights at Barnham on the A134, about ¼-mile west of the junction); Kennett station.

Public transport: Central Trains to Thetford station; Anglia Railways to Kennett station. Infrequent buses from Thetford and Bury St Edmunds to Euston. Buses between Newmarket and Bury stop at Kentford and intersect the route just to the west of the village where it crosses the A14.

Cycle hire: High Lodge Cycle Hire, Thetford Forest (01842 815078 day, 0589 100831 after 6pm).

Below: The Icknield Way route near Icklingham.

Distance: About 20 miles one way.

Maps: OS Landrangers 144 (Thetford & Breckland), 155 (Bury St Edmunds & Sudbury), and 154 (Cambridge & Newmarket). Icknield Way leaflets, available from Tourist Information Centres.

Surfaces and gradients: Gradients are mostly gentle. Most of the route is across the Brecks — open heathland with some forest sections and fields. The ground is often very sandy, so the surfaces are firm and well-drained, but expect some muddy bits after heavy rain.

Roads and crossing points: Very short section on the A134; B1106 crossed near Elveden. At Icklingham there is a very short section on the A1101. The main street at Tuddenham is a class C road, and cyclists must follow it for almost ½-mile before coming to a quieter lane. If going to Kennett (it is possible to continue past this, and link with Route 10) there is a short stretch on the B1085.

National Cycle Network connections: The Ipswich to Cambridge route (513) will intersect the Icknield Way, as will the Bury to Thetford route (135).

Refreshments: Thetford has all facilities. Pubs at Icklingham (two), Tuddenham (also a village shop), Kennett End and Kentford.

ROUTE INSTRUCTIONS
From Euston follow the Icknield Way signs along what was once the London Road, going in a southwesterly direction. At the A134

go right then left almost at once, and pick up the excellent track across Thetford Heath. (If you are starting from the Air Products depot — actually the site of Barnham station — go south along the signed byway, deviating slightly only to avoid the works at Little Heath. This will intersect the Icknield Way about two miles to the south and is clearly signed.) Be sure to follow the 'Icknield Way Riders' Route' signs where there is a choice.

Follow the signs to the B1106. (If you approach from the other direction, it is very easy to miss the right turn off the main track soon after passing the farm buildings here.) Cross the road and continue to follow the excellent track until the Elveden Monument hoves into view. This is on the other side of the A11 — turn left at the byway 'crossroads', there being no Icknield Way sign.

Right: Thomas Paine is commemorated by this statue in the centre of Thetford. This is one possible starting point for the Icknield Way route to Kennett and Newmarket.

Continue on this track: it is a steady descent if going southwest. At Icklingham turn left onto the A1101 (take care), and right just before the church (about 150yd). Cross the River Lark at Temple Bridge and continue to Tuddenham.

The Icknield Way footpath continues across the main road and quickly turns into a bridleway. However, the cycle route turns right and goes along the main road (past the pub). After about ½-mile, ignore the left turn and go straight ahead. Take the next track on the left (under ½-mile), and follow this lane to Herringswell, turning left towards the church, where it rejoins the footpath. Almost opposite is a signed track on the right heading almost due south. Follow this either to the A14 (about 2 miles), where you can continue along the Icknield Way to Gazeley, Cheveley and westwards, or along the B1506 to Kennett station (turn right at Kennett End onto the B1085). The B1506 is busy, being the old A45. An alternative route is to turn right off the Icknield Way about ¾-mile short of the A14 onto an unsigned byway. It starts well but is later partly blocked by dumping. It is possible to negotiate this and emerge at Kentford Heath. Go straight ahead on the road, cut the next corner using a signed byway on the left, left again, left in Kennett, and left onto the B1085.

Left: Icknield Way signing in typical Breckland countryside. This point marks the junction of the Way proper and the route from Barnham.

ROUTE 8
EUSTON TO KENNETT

ROUTE 9

NORWICH

PLACES OF INTEREST ALONG THE ROUTE

Too many attractions in Norwich to list them all, but the following are a few highlights. The cathedral is a major landmark, and the castle dominates the city and houses a splendid museum. It overlooks the Castle Mall shopping centre, which is almost entirely underground.

Starting point: Norwich (Thorpe) station.

Parking: Many car parks in Norwich, but the situation is difficult and expensive on

Norwich market is famous for its myriad stalls selling every imaginable product; nearby is the Royal Arcade, taking shopping back into an age of greater elegance. City Hall overlooks the market and the Guildhall, the latter now housing the Tourist Information Centre (01603 666071). The celebrated Theatre Royal is nearby, and the adjacent Assembly Rooms offer further exhibitions and refreshments, and have recently been rebuilt following serious fire damage. Assuming that you arrive by train, it is worth stopping a moment to savour the fine architecture of Thorpe station, recently completely refurbished.

weekdays. There are park-and-ride sites at Harford, the airport and Postwick. Use public transport if possible.

Below: Bishop's Bridge, Norwich, the only remaining medieval bridge left in the city. It is recently restored and traffic-free.

Public transport: Anglia Railways' and Central Trains' services to Norwich. Buses from all parts of Norfolk, north Suffolk and elsewhere (country buses mostly go to and from the bus station in Surrey Street).

Cycle hire: Anglia Bike Centre, 72a Gloucester Street (01603 632467); Freewheel, 75 Prince of Wales Road, Norwich NR1 1DG (01603 610072).

Maps: OS Landranger 134 (Norwich & The Broads). Outdoor Leisure 40 (The Broads) shows much of the city on the northeast side. Sustrans Fakenham to Harwich, panels 1 and 2. Norwich Cycle Route map (free), from Tourist Information Centre in the Guildhall, or call the Cycling Officer, Norwich City Council (01603 215515).

Surfaces and gradients: No significant gradients. Metalled surfaces.

Roads and crossing points: It is difficult to get through Norwich without going on the roads, but many routes have cycle lanes or segregated tracks.

National Cycle Network connections: Norwich is on the Harwich to Hull route.

Refreshments: Too many to name! Norwich has a huge selection of pubs and tea shops: it is a major regional centre and has all facilities.

ROUTE INSTRUCTIONS
This route gets you from the station to the Marriott's Way. There are many other ways through the city and to its surroundings.

From Norwich station turn right into Riverside Road (busy), so that the river is on your left. After about ¼-mile turn left over Bishop's Bridge (traffic-free — the only medieval bridge left in Norwich). Go straight ahead along Bishopgate, with the cathedral ahead. Pass the Adam & Eve pub, said to be the oldest in the city. Continue past the Law Courts (not traffic-free, but quiet). Cross the main road (pelican on

Below: Cycle parking near Fye Bridge, Norwich. The area is traffic-calmed.

Above: Norwich is dominated by the castle, which now houses a splendid museum. Castle Meadow skirts the castle mound, and is experimentally open only to buses, taxis and cycles.

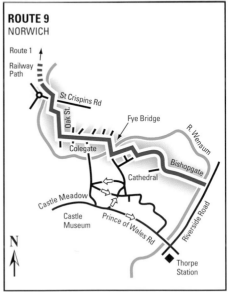

ROUTE 9
NORWICH

right) in front of the Wig & Pen pub and go down Bedding Lane by the pub. (Don't try Piggs Lane — it is cobbled!)

Follow this lane (Quayside) to Fye Bridge and turn right, then left into Colegate. Continue along this street, and cross Duke Street at the pelican, wheeling your bike across. Colegate continues straight ahead, although motorised traffic cannot. Turn right into Oak Street and continue to the main road, turning left on to the off-road shared track. Cross the road at the pelican, and follow the Marriott's Way or Railway Path signs, off to the right.

ICKNIELD WAY — BALSHAM TO NEWMARKET

PLACES OF INTEREST ALONG THE ROUTE

This is rolling countryside, and in spring and summer it abounds with wildlife: birds, insects, wildflowers, and as the autumn wears on, lapwings move from the coast to the fields and meadows to forage for the winter.

Nearer to Newmarket the influence of horse racing becomes stronger, with stables, studs and rides. The National Horse Racing Museum and Tours, in the High Street, traces the story of the people and the horses involved in racing, from its royal origins to its modern jockeys and trainers. Tours are led by experts on the equine world, and include training on the gallops, the horses' swimming pool, a training yard, and mares and foals at a top stud. It is open March to October, except Mondays (01638 667333). The National Stud (01638 666789) offers guided tours, by appointment only, and is open March to August, and race days in September and October.

Starting point(s): Fairly easy ride. Horseheath (see Route 11), Balsham. See also Cambridge (Route 12), and Icknield Way — Kennett to Thetford (Route 8).

Parking: Balsham post office.

Public transport: Anglia Railways to Newmarket. Infrequent bus service from Cambridge to Balsham.

Cycle hire: Geoff's Bike Hire, 65 Devonshire Road, Cambridge

(01223 365629); Cambridge Recycles, On the Roundabout, Newnham Road, Cambridge CB3 9EN (01223 506035); H. Drake, 56-60 Hills Road, (01223 363468); Roses Cycles, 173 High Street, Chesterton (01223 356162/564607); Cycle King, 195 Mill Road, Cambridge (01223 212222).

Distance: About 13 miles one way.

Maps: OS Landranger 154 (Cambridge & Newmarket)

Surfaces and gradients: Fairly easy ride. Surfaces generally firm. There are a few sections where it can be muddy, and the occasional short grassy stretch. The countryside is rolling, so there are long pulls uphill in several places.

Roads and crossing points: Short section in Balsham along the B1052, also used for about a mile through Brinkley. B1061 is used briefly at Burrough Green. Access into Newmarket is via a minor road for nearly 2 miles.

National Cycle Network connections:
Routes from Harlow to Ely and March, and from Ipswich to Milton Keynes cross at Cambridge.

Refreshments:
Pubs and shops at Balsham, Brinkley and Stetchworth; pubs at Burrough Green and Woodditton. Newmarket has all facilities.

ROUTE INSTRUCTIONS
From Balsham post office, go west along the B1052 (see Route 11 if you wish to start at Horseheath; adds about 3 miles to the ride). Take care to follow 'Icknield Way Riders Route' signs where they exist. Turn right off the main road: there are two large horse chestnut trees growing on a triangle of grass at the junction. Follow this track for some 4 miles — it undulates quite a lot — and is well signed. It emerges onto the B1052 and there is no choice but to turn left and follow this into Brinkley. Continuing northward, the path leaves the B1052 about half a mile from the village:

Previous page: Newmarket is an interesting town and the home of the Jockey Club. This fine clock tower stands at the north end of the main street.

Below: At Camois Hall Farm, the Icknield Way diverts from its original track, rejoining it shortly afterwards.

Above: Approaching Balsham from the south. This section of the Icknield Way provides a connection with the Roman Road.

turn right opposite the road to Westley Waterless. This a wide grassy track with an asphalted path along one side. Follow this to the B1061 at Burrough Green and turn left, then right shortly after. This next byway can be muddy. Turn left at the lane (very quiet) and right after about ¾-mile onto a bridleway, also muddy.

Go right onto the busier road at the end. Turn left at the water tower onto a good track that descends quite steeply. Approaching the farm at the bottom, the path has been diverted onto a grassy track to the right, rejoining the original alignment further on. Continue to a staggered road crossing. At this point you have a choice:

1. The Icknield Way signs direct you to the right; take the first left (about ½-mile) and go along a minor road into Newmarket,

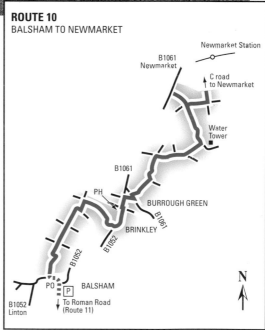

ROUTE 10
BALSHAM TO NEWMARKET

coming out quite near the station.
2. Go straight ahead for another mile on an excellent bridleway, but enter Newmarket after 1½ miles on the B1061.

THE ROMAN ROAD

PLACES OF INTEREST ALONG THE ROUTE

This may look straight and therefore dull on the map — not a bit of it! This is a varied and fascinating route, rich in wildlife.

Starting point(s): Horseheath, off A1307 Haverhill-Cambridge road. It is also possible to start at the Cambridge end, where parking is available.

Parking: Very limited: at start of ride or at the roadside in the village.

Public transport: Train to Cambridge (WAGN, Anglia or Central Trains) or Great Shelford (WAGN). Bus service Haverhill-Cambridge.

Haverhill Local History Centre is in the Town Hall, open Tuesdays to Saturdays all year. It has photographs, memorabilia and archive material. Chilford Hall Vineyard is the largest in East Anglia, open daily from Good Friday to the end of September. Wandlebury Country Park is signed at the Cambridge end and is set in the Gog Magog Hills. This is an area of ancient legends: Gog and Magog feature in the Bible and Koran, as well as Arthurian and medieval tales.

Cycle hire: Geoff's Bike Hire, 65 Devonshire Road, Cambridge (01223 365629); Cambridge Recycles, On the Roundabout, Newnham Road, Cambridge CB3 9EN (01223 506035); H. Drake, 56-60 Hills Road (01223 363468); Roses Cycles, 173 High Street, Chesterton (01223 356162/564607); Cycle King, 195 Mill Road, Cambridge (01223 212222).

Distance: About 11 miles.

Maps: Landranger 154 (Cambridge & Newmarket).

Surfaces and gradients: Fairly easy, except one challenging section (see text). Surface varies: fine gravel, stony, may be slightly overgrown in places; some firm woodland tracks. Gradients generally level or easy.

Roads and crossing points: Two minor roads, plus B1052. A11(T) crossed by bridge.

Refreshments: Balsham has pubs and shops, but is a 1½-mile diversion. Possible to divert into Linton, also with pubs and shops. Cambridge has all facilities.

ROUTE INSTRUCTIONS

Start of route is where the Horseheath to West Wickham road intersects the Roman Road: signed westwards as a bridleway. Slightly overgrown initially, it soon widens into a track along a headland: this sort of variety occurs all along the route. Pass Streetly Hall on the right and cross a minor road and pick up the Roman Road proper. The variety of wildflowers and insect life is quite astonishing on this next section.

Opposite page: 'I know a bank where the wild thyme blows' said Oberon in A Midsummer Night's Dream. By the time the Bard wrote these words, wild thyme had been growing along the Roman Road for well over a millennium, and it remains a rich source of wildlife.

Below: The Roman Road near Horseheath.

About a mile further the track becomes more wooded and a branch goes right (poorly waymarked) for the Icknield Way and Balsham. Continue straight ahead for the Roman Road. Parking possible at crossing of B1052; Linton is about 1½ miles on the left. Ignore the 'Riders Route' signs and continue straight ahead. After the next minor road crossing the route becomes overgrown, but still passable. This is the most challenging section.

Some three miles further on, the A11(T) is crossed by a modern bridge; continue in the same direction and ignore other signs. The route ends at a car park, turning right to meet the Cambridge to Fulbourn road. The entry to the route here is clearly marked 'Public Byway — Roman Road'.

Above: The Roman Road is overgrown in places, but still easily cycled. It is undulating, with a hard chalky surface.

ROUTE 11
THE ROMAN ROAD

Cambridge   Fulbourn
P
A1307
Cambridge
A11
Norwich
B1052
BALSHAM
PH
Icknield Way (To Route 10)
STREETLY END
A11
to M11
LINTON
PH   HORSEHEATH
N
B1052
Saffron Walden
A1307
Haverhill

CAMBRIDGE

PLACES OF INTEREST ALONG THE ROUTE

Cambridge is one of the most vibrant cities in Britain: a centre of industry and academia, as well as a major regional shopping centre. Its attractions for visitors are too numerous to mention; unfortunately, it suffers from serious traffic problems. The city has many museums, galleries and a range of architecture going back many centuries. Full details of opening times and admission charges are available from the Tourist Information Centre in Wheeler Street (01223 322640). This is a list of some of the attractions: Fitzwilliam Museum (paintings, antiquities, ceramics), Folk Museum (Cambridgeshire bygones), Kettles Yard Gallery (modern art), Scott Polar Research Institute, Sedgwick Museum (geological), University Museum of Archaeology and Anthropology, Museum of Zoology, Whipple Museum of Science, University Museum of Classical Archaeology, The Backs, Botanic Gardens, Castle Mound, Jesus Green, Cambridge University Library. It is possible for visitors to walk through most of the college courts and visit the chapels, although they are private places for scholars and staff. Some make an admission charge, and most are closed during the exam periods from mid-April to the end of June. Punts can be hired at Quayside (by Magdalene Bridge) or the Mill Pond, by Mill Lane. There are many churches which are open to visitors.

Above: Punting is one of the popular pastimes in Cambridge and punts can be hired here, where Silver Street crosses the River Cam.

Above: Cambridge is noted for its colleges: this is Corpus Christi.

Starting point: Cambridge station.

Parking: Very difficult. Travel by public transport is strongly recommended.

Public transport: West Anglia Great Northern train services from London, Ely and King's Lynn. Central Trains from Birmingham, Norwich and Stansted Airport. Anglia Railways from Ipswich. Buses and coaches from all parts of East Anglia.

Cycle hire: Geoff's Bike Hire, 65 Devonshire Road, Cambridge (01223 365629); Cambridge Recycles, On the Roundabout, Newnham Road, Cambridge CB3 9EN (01223 506035); H. Drake, 56-60 Hills Road (01223 363468); Roses Cycles, 173 High Street, Chesterton (01223 356162/564607); Cycle King, 195 Mill Road, Cambridge (01223 212222).

Maps: OS Landranger 154 (Cambridge & Newmarket); Cycle Routes In and Around Cambridge, and the general information leaflet on Cambridge (from the Tourist Information Centre, or Cambridgeshire County Council, 01223 717445).

Surfaces and gradients: Almost all metalled surfaces. No significant gradients, except the rail bridge.

Roads and crossing points: Some off-road provision, but much is by means of cycle lanes and pedestrian shared-use paths.

National Cycle Network connections: Cambridge is at the junction of routes from London (via the Lea Valley) to King's Lynn, and Felixstowe to the Midlands.

Right: Cambridge has many measures to help cyclists. At this locaion they are allowed to cross where cars are not, and special traffic lights are provided.

Refreshments: Cambridge has all facilities.

ROUTE INSTRUCTIONS

From the railway station turn right (follow the signs to the city centre). The route initially goes through the car park and emerges by the cycle bridge which spans the railway and provides an invaluable short cut. Access the city centre by turning either left (via Devonshire Road, Lyndewood Road, Gresham Road and Parker's Piece) or right via St Barnabas Road, Gwydir Street and the Grafton Centre. Signing of cycle routes is generally good.

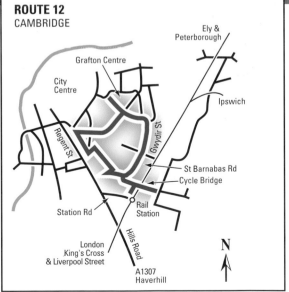

ROUTE 12
CAMBRIDGE

Ely & Peterborough

Grafton Centre

City Centre

Ipswich

Regent St

Gwydir St

St Barnabas Rd

Cycle Bridge

Station Rd

Rail Station

Hills Road

London King's Cross & Liverpool Street

A1307 Haverhill

N

ROUTE 13

PETERBOROUGH AND THE NENE VALLEY

PLACES OF INTEREST ALONG THE ROUTE

Nene Valley Railway from Peterborough

Starting point(s): Peterborough station; Orton Mere station (see below).

Parking: Multi-storey car park at Queensgate shopping centre; Ferry Meadows.

Public transport: Train services to Peterborough station (GNER from London, Scotland and the north of England; WAGN from London and intermediate stations;

(NVR station) to Wansford (talking timetable 01780 784440); Cathedral: started in 1118 and consecrated in 1238, in the city centre and easily accessible by bike (01733 343342); Museum and Art Gallery, Priestgate, open Tuesday-Saturday (01733 343329); Flag Fen Bronze Age Archaeology Park; many wildlife reserves such as Ferry Meadows. Details of all of them from the Tourist Information Centre in Bridge Street (01733 452336).

Central from Norwich, Cambridge and the Midlands; Anglia from Ipswich). Bus services from a wide area serve the bus station, which is close to the rail station; Nene Valley Railway offers seasonal services westwards towards Wansford.

Cycle hire: Terry Wright Cycles, 39 Bridge Street, Deeping St James (01778 343433); Bristows, 46 Church Drive, Orton Waterville (01733 231755).

Above: Much of the centre of Peterborough has been pedestrianised and most of it is open to cyclists. This is the Guildhall.

Maps: OS Landranger 142 (Peterborough); Pathfinder 918 (Peterborough [South] and Wansford) is the most useful, but it appears on three other sheets as well — 897, 898 and 919! Peterborough Sports, Leisure & Cycling Routes (60p in 1998) — available from the Tourist Information Centre in Bridge Street.

Surfaces and gradients: Very easy riding. Almost invariably metalled surfaces, with a few hard-surfaced tracks; no significant gradients.

Roads and crossing points: Occasionally necessary to cross a main road to get from the city centre to the route out to Ferry Meadows. Peterborough generally has an excellent network of off-road cycle tracks penetrating the city centre and allowing access to the surrounding countryside.

Refreshments: Peterborough has all facilities. Café at Ferry Meadows Country Park, and sometimes at Orton Mere station when the Nene Valley Railway is operating.

ROUTE INSTRUCTIONS
From the railway station turn right and follow the path to the right, just before the road into the car park. This will bring you into the system of cycle paths. At the junction follow the appropriate signs. The route into the city centre is via Cowgate. NOTE that there is no cycling in Bridge Street between 9am and 6pm, although most other parts of the centre are accessible by bike.

Possible routes to the Ferry Meadows Country Park, none of which is perfect:

1. Go along Bridge Street (wheel bike, see above) and cross the main road at the traffic lights. Continue straight ahead; cyclists keep to the left. Turn left before the next main road and follow the path past the

Opposite page: The path out to Ferry Meadows Country Park follows the course of the Nene Valley Railway and gives an easy ride from the city centre.

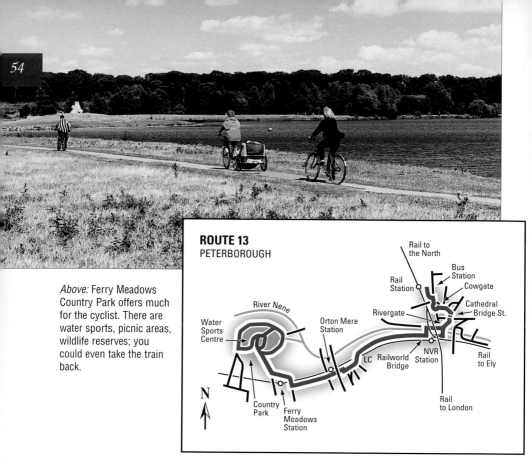

Above: Ferry Meadows Country Park offers much for the cyclist. There are water sports, picnic areas, wildlife reserves; you could even take the train back.

ROUTE 13
PETERBOROUGH

Court House; right immediately with the Lido straight ahead. Bear left at the Key Theatre and continue to the riverbank. Turn right (beware — the edge is unprotected). This will bring you out on the main road; cross the river and follow signs to the right.

2. Alternatively, having crossed the road at the end of Bridge Street, look for an archway on the right headed 'Rivergate'. Go through and follow signs for 'Railworld'. Either go over the bridge (it has shallow steps at both ends) and turn westwards for the Nene Valley railway station, or right and go along the north bank of the river, crossing the Railworld bridge further along. Cycling is not allowed by this route until you get to the riverbank.

Follow the path to the Nene Valley Railway station and continue past it: the path is right next to the railway line,

securely fenced. It crosses the track at the junction with the Fletton loop line; continue roughly parallel to the railway, taking the second right and then left, emerging at Orton Mere station. Don't cross the railway here, but follow signs to Orton Meadows, Ferry Meadows and Lynch Wood.

Continue parallel to the railway, again crossing it, and passing Ferry Meadows station. Bear right into the Country Park (many attractions, especially water sports). The lake is easily circumnavigated by bike, with several alternative routes back to Peterborough. If you cycle round to the opposite side of the lake and turn left (northwards) you will come to Ferry Bridge and have the choice of a number of signed off-road routes to Marholm and Bretton via Milton Park, and a series of routes designated the 'Green Wheel'.

THE RIVER GREAT OUSE

PLACES OF INTEREST ALONG THE ROUTE

Downham Market is an interesting town, with an unusual black and white clock tower. Denver Sluice, just south of the starting point of this ride, is the tidal limit of the Great Ouse river. The area between the Old and New Bedford rivers, created over 200 years ago by the building of the drainage schemes, is an internationally renowned area for wildfowl. The 'Collectors World of Eric St John Foti' hosts a large collection of bygones, and is just to the west of the Great Ouse bridge. The Tourist Information Centre is in Bridge Street (01366 698992).

The whole ride is good for viewing bird life, especially waders when the tide is low. King's Lynn has many attractions: see Route 6 for details.

Starting point(s): Downham Market or Wiggenhall St Germans.

Parking: Downham Market town centre.

Public transport: WAGN railway to Downham Market.

Cycle hire: Bircham Windmill (01485 578393).

Distance: About 8 miles one way. It is possible to extend the ride southwards along either the River Great Ouse or the Hundred Foot Drain.

Maps: Landrangers 131 (Boston & Spalding), 132 (Northwest Norfolk), 143 (Ely & Wisbech).

Left: Downham Market is the starting point for the route along the River Great Ouse, although it is equally possible to go inland. The unusual clock tower is a feature of the town.

Surfaces and gradients: Fairly easy ride. No significant gradients. Surface generally either hard and grassy, or compacted sandy ballast.

Roads and crossing points: Minor roads at Stowbridge and Wiggenhall St Mary Magdalen.

National Cycle Network connections: Route 1 crosses the River Great Ouse at Wiggenhall St Germans.

Refreshments: Downham Market has all facilities. Pubs at Stowbridge, Wiggenhall St Mary Magdalen and Wiggenhall St Germans.

ROUTE INSTRUCTIONS

From Downham Market station go along the A1122 towards Outwell and Wisbech. Go over the first bridge and continue to the second. There is access to the paths, which are on the river walls, on both sides. Use the one on the Downham Market (east) side and head north, which has recently been signed as the 'Fen Rivers Way'. Continue northwards, keeping to the river wall and the path.

About half a mile short of Wiggenhall St Mary Magdalen a disused railway bridge carried the former Magdalen Road to Wisbech line over the river. Be sure to transfer to the river wall here. Go past some houses, and either stay on the grassy wall or descend to the unmetalled track. Cross the minor road and continue northwards. Take care when approaching Wiggenhall St Germans, as the path emerges in the garden at the Crown & Anchor pub. Although it continues towards King's Lynn, it is not possible to cycle beyond this point. If you wish to get there, follow the NCN Route 1 signs.

Below: The ruins of a church, now under restoration, at Wiggenhall St Peter.

Above: Typical Fenland country, with the Great Ouse constrained by high banks. The excellent surface of the track has recently been renewed. The relief channel is out of sight to the right of the picture.

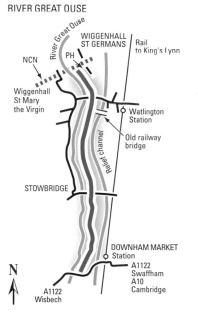

ROUTE 14
RIVER GREAT OUSE

River Great Ouse

WIGGENHALL
ST GERMANS

Rail
to King's Lynn

NCN

PH

Wiggenhall
St Mary
the Virgin

Watlington
Station

Relief channel

Old railway
bridge

STOWBRIDGE

DOWNHAM MARKET
Station

A1122
Swaffham
A10
Cambridge

N

A1122
Wisbech

HADLEIGH RAILWAY WALK

PLACES OF INTEREST ALONG THE ROUTE

The ride follows the course of part of the former railway between Bentley and Hadleigh. Only a short section is available for walking and cycling.

Hadleigh is a very pleasant old Suffolk country town and the administrative centre of Babergh District Council. It has much fine architecture, including St Mary's church, Deanery Tower, Guildhall and adjoining Town Hall, all Grade 1 listed buildings, and the old Corn Exchange, which now serves as the area Social Services office. There is an admission charge for the Guildhall, which includes a guided tour (Thursday and Sunday afternoons, June-August). A path along the River Brett leads to the 500-year-old red brick Toppesfield Bridge. There is a market on Fridays.

Hadleigh Wet Meadows are traditionally farmed, and accessible from the railway walk. Wolves Wood is an RSPB reserve off the A1071. Kersey Pottery has handmade stoneware by Dorothy Gorst and Fred Bramham, and is open Tuesdays to Fridays between Easter and Christmas.

Starting point(s): Hadleigh old railway station, Station Road, or Raydon Wood old railway station, on the road from Raydon to Hintlesham.

Parking: Limited, at each end; also in Hadleigh town.

Public transport: Frequent bus services to Ipswich and Sudbury also to Colchester.

Cycle hire: Suffolk Cycle Centre, Sudbury (01787 310940); Cycles Store, Sudbury (01787 881810); Bicycle Doctor & Hire, 18 Bartholomew Street, Ipswich

(01473 259853); Bartons Bicycles,
5 Marriotts Walk, Stowmarket (01449
677195).

Distance: About 2¼ miles each way.

Maps: Landranger 155 (Bury St Edmunds &
Sudbury). Sustrans 'Fakenham to Harwich'
sheet, panel 5.

Surfaces and gradients: A very easy ride.
No gradients. Surfaces very good.

Roads and crossing points: None.

National Cycle Network connections:
Part of the Harwich to Hull route.

Refreshments: Hadleigh has all facilities.

ROUTE INSTRUCTIONS
Not needed. Join the path at either end and
follow the clear track to the other.

Opposite page: The Hadleigh Railway Walk now forms part of the National Cycle Network. It follows the
course of part of the old railway from Bentley.

Above: Hadleigh Railway Walk, near Hadleigh.

Above: Hadleigh Guildhall, one of
many historic buildings in the town.

ROUTE 15
HADLEIGH RAILWAY WALK

A1071
Ipswich

Bus
Station

HADLEIGH

Old Station

B1070
East Bergholt

P

Raydon Wood
old station

N

RENDLESHAM FOREST

PLACES OF INTEREST ALONG THE ROUTE

Rendlesham Forest itself is of great interest. It has much wildlife and excellent facilities for a very wide range of visitors, including a surfaced trail for wheelchair users. Butley Pottery is in Mill Lane (01394 450875); free admission.

Starting point: Phoenix Trail car park at Rendlesham Forest, or car park nearer to B1084.

Parking: See above.

Public transport: Very limited bus service Ipswich-Woodbridge-Melton-Orford. Anglia Railways to Melton, about 5 miles from the route (further to the car parks).

Cycle hire: Pedal Power at the Phoenix Trail car park (01473 610500 or 0378 183814 [mobile]); Byways Bicycles, Priory Farm, Priory Lane, Darsham, Saxmundham IP17 3QD (01728 668764).

Distance: Short route about 4 miles; long route about 9 miles.

Maps: OS Landranger 156 (Saxmundham & Aldeburgh), 169 (Ipswich & The Naze); Cycling in the Forest: Rendlesham Forest (from Forest Enterprises Tangham office, 01394 450164).

Surfaces and gradients: The short route is mostly forest tracks. Long route has nearly 3 miles along the C road through Sutton Common. Some short but steep gradients.

Roads and crossing points: Short route: none; long route: see above. If connecting with the Tunstall Forest route, there is a crossing of the B1084, and another very brief stretch on it at Butley.

National Cycle Network connections: The Felixstowe to Orford section of the

Previous page: A typical track through mature pine woodland in Rendlesham Forest.

Below: There is an excellent off-road connection between Rendlesham and Tunstall forests: this is near Chillesford.

Harwich to Hull route passes Butley.

Refreshments: The Tangham office sells drinks; Butley Oyster pub, Butley Pottery tea room & restaurant.

ROUTE INSTRUCTIONS

Follow the waymarks from the car parks.

There is a good connection to Tunstall Forest (Route 17): start either from the Phoenix Trail car park, or the one nearer the B1084, and go north towards the main road. Turn left past the air base fence along a good, marked track. When it curves left, go straight ahead (waymarked). Follow this very good

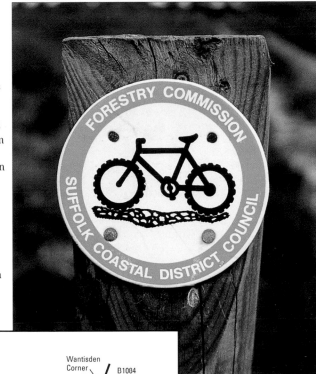

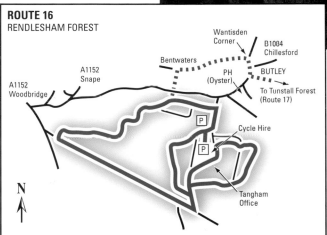

ROUTE 16
RENDLESHAM FOREST

Above: These waymarks were produced to mark the Three Forests Way, linking Rendlesham, Tunstall and Dunwich, and can still be found in abundance.

heathland track, and at the next Y-junction go right (follow the old waymarks). After 200yd or so, cross the B1084 (take care). Continue straight ahead, crossing several junctions. When you come to a T-junction, with a big fence in front of you (the former Bentwaters air base), go right. This is a good track. Keep on it, past Staverton

Caravan Park, and emerge onto a metalled road. (This went to the air base, but is now more or less traffic-free.) Turn right. At Wantisden Corner follow the road round to the right, joining the B1084. The Butley Oyster pub is about 200yd ahead; now see Route 17.

TUNSTALL FOREST

PLACES OF INTEREST ALONG THE ROUTE

Starting point(s): Butley Oyster; Froize Arms at Chillesford.

Parking: Very limited. On B1078 where the route crosses; Tunstall Common; either pub.

Public transport: Anglia Railways to Wickham Market station: about four miles to Tunstall Common. Bus services very limited.

Cycle hire: Phoenix Trail car park (01394 450164); Byways Bicycles, Priory Farm, Priory Lane, Darsham, Saxmundham IP17 3QD (01728 668764).

Another Forest Enterprises route, in conjunction with Suffolk Coastal District Council. The start is shown as the Oyster pub at Butley, which provides a connection with Route 16 (Rendlesham Forest). The main interest is the wildlife — birds, dragonflies, butterflies and other insects, and flowers. Butley Pottery.

Distance: About 9 miles, circular.

Maps: OS Landranger 156 (Saxmundham & Aldeburgh). Sustrans Fakenham to Harwich, panel 4.

Surfaces and gradients: Fairly easy ride. Mostly forest tracks, variable quality, some quite stony. Used by horses in many places. Few significant gradients.

Roads and crossing points: Between the Butley Oyster and Chillesford, uses a very quiet metalled lane; otherwise two crossings of the B1078, two of the B1084.

Below: A track along the edge of Tunstall Forest.

Above: The eastern part of Suffolk is naturally sandy and if left to itself will regrow silver birch, which slowly replaces the brightly coloured heaths.

National Cycle Network connections: Butley to Chillesford is on the Harwich-Hull route.

Refreshments: The Oyster, Butley and Froize Arms, Chillesford; both have excellent real ale and good food; the latter is very expensive.

ROUTE INSTRUCTIONS

From the Butley Oyster go north along the B1084, turning right almost immediately. Follow NCN Route 1 sign. At the B1084 ignore NCN sign and go straight ahead onto a track, steep for a short distance. Turn right at the next crossway, with Chillesford church on the left. Continue about 2 miles on an excellent track, mostly through woodland: look out for butterflies and green woodpeckers! Cross the B1078 at Tunstall Common (signed on the far side as a footpath) and shortly bear right onto a wide sandy track which approaches from the village. There is much horse riding along here. After a mile or so pick up the cycling waymarks and turn right, off the main track: the cycle route is grassy. Continue to the next track and turn left, now going eastwards. Continue across the next two tracks and right almost immediately at the next cross track. Turn right at the next cross onto a stony track. After about ¼-mile fork left off the main track, following the waymarks. Keep going to the B1078 (limited parking possible) and continue straight ahead. After 200yd turn right (straight ahead to the Froize Arms). Continue until a major cross-track and turn left. Continue as far as the next track and go past the barrier and turn left to rejoin the original route heading back towards Butley. NOTE: from the Froize Arms take the track opposite (clearly signed) and follow the waymarks. Be careful, as the main track goes left just before entering the forest: watch for waymarks and keep straight ahead.

Above: Part of this route goes through Tunstall Common, to the east of the village. Refreshments are available at the Green Man pub.

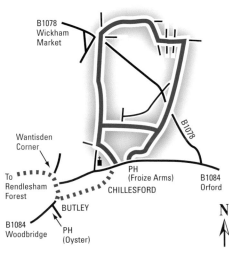

ROUTE 17
TUNSTALL FOREST

B1078
Wickham
Market

B1078

Wantisden
Corner

To
Rendlesham
Forest

PH
(Froize Arms)

CHILLESFORD

B1084
Orford

BUTLEY

B1084
Woodbridge

PH
(Oyster)

N

DUNWICH FOREST

PLACES OF INTEREST ALONG THE ROUTE

Dunwich was once England's greatest port, and legends abound. It is said that one can hear the bells of drowned churches tolling beneath the waves; what is certain is that the coastline was once more than a mile further out to sea. Little is now left apart from St James' church, outside the old city walls, the ruins of Greyfriars Priory, the Beach Café, the Ship Inn (the latter two specialise in local fish and chips) and an

excellent award-winning museum (open daily April to September, and at other times, 01728 648796, admission free). Dunwich Forest has much wildlife of interest and borders Westleton Heath nature reserve. Access is also relatively easy to Walberswick and Southwold, both of which have great charm. Southwold has an interesting museum, a pier and a fine church, and is home to Adnams brewery. The most direct connection in summer is via a small ferry, but it is also possible to go via a bridge over the River Blyth which replaces the swing bridge once used by the Southwold Railway, the trackbed of which can be followed most of the way to Blythburgh.

Starting point(s): Dunwich beach car park; Forest Enterprises car park off the Blythburgh-Dunwich road (nearest to the B1125, on southwest side of road). There is another car park on the other side of the road, nearer to Dunwich village.

Parking: See above.

Public transport: No significant bus service to Dunwich. Anglia Railways

Left: St James' Church, well outside the original city walls, is now the sole survivor of many. A buttress of the last church in the city, All Saints', was re-erected here after the last remains of the tower finally went over the cliff in 1922.

to Darsham, about 5 miles.

Cycle hire: Byways Bicycles, Priory Farm, Priory Lane, Darsham, Saxmundham IP17 3QD (01728 668764).

Distance: About 5 miles circular, plus connections to Dunwich village. Also connects with Route 22 (Dunwich to Thorpeness).

Maps: OS Landranger 156 (Saxmundham & Aldeburgh); Pathfinder 966 (Southwold & Halesworth); Forest Enterprises 'Three Forests Cycle Trail' leaflet.

Surfaces and gradients: Fairly easy ride. Mostly forest tracks, of which some may be muddy and some stony. Some short steep gradients.

Roads and crossing points: One short stretch on the Blythburgh-Dunwich road, and one other crossing. The route into Dunwich village goes on the road for the final half mile.

National Cycle Network connections: The nearest approach is at Green Farm, west of Darsham, by the Harwich to Hull route.

Refreshments: Beach Café at Dunwich, and Ship Inn.

ROUTE INSTRUCTIONS
Starting from the Forest Enterprises car park nearest Blythburgh, continue along the entrance road, barred to cars. Almost at once take the signed right turn onto the forest track. Follow the route straight ahead, crossing a number of other tracks and going from pine forest to replanted heathland. Go right (signed) on to another track, and cross a minor road. Pass the old ballast pit, then take the signed right turn. Cross the road, taking the grassy track

Above: Dunwich Forest has much to offer the cyclist and has good off-road access to the village.

opposite: can be overgrown, good surface. Go left onto a better track, going steeply downhill — can be sandy here — and enter woodland. The main track goes straight ahead, but turn right (signed as a 'permit horse trail' and easy to miss). Go left at the T-junction, pick up cycle route signs, going right. The path from here can be overgrown — follow the signs. Eventually emerge onto a wide stony track: continue along this, crossing a prominent vehicle-access track protected by barriers, and coming to another barrier, barring vehicle access from another track. Here you have a choice.

1. Either cross the barrier onto this track: it takes you down to Dunwich, emerging near St James' church, about ¼-mile from the pub and beach.

2. Or pass the barrier and remain in the forest itself, turning right at the next T-junction (unsigned). Follow this track past a car park, turning right, then left at the T-junction. Follow signs to the cross-tracks, going left. Go left onto the road (take care), and come to the car park on the right after about 150yd.

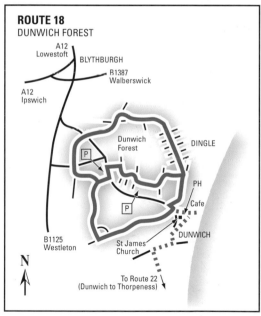

ROUTE 18
DUNWICH FOREST

A12 Lowestoft

BLYTHBURGH

B1387 Walberswick

A12 Ipswich

Dunwich Forest

DINGLE

P

PH

Cafe

P

DUNWICH

B1125 Westleton

St James' Church

N

To Route 22 (Dunwich to Thorpeness)

Above: Greyfriars Priory, Dunwich. The ruins can still be viewed today: the encroaching sea has not yet claimed them.

ROUTE 19

DEBENHAM AND EARL SOHAM

PLACES OF INTEREST ALONG THE ROUTE

Earl Soham and Debenham are interesting, old and picturesque Suffolk towns. Earl Soham now has only one pub, the Victoria, which is the home of the Earl Soham

brewery. Saxtead windmill has been fully restored. It is an 18th century post mill with roundhouse and is open Mondays to Saturdays, April to September.

At Debenham there is Carter's Teapot Pottery, one of Britain's top teapot makers. There is a viewing area and shop, and it is open all year round. Debenham also has many antique shops. For railway enthusiasts, the Mid Suffolk Light Railway museum is a short distance away at Wetheringsett and is open Sundays and Bank Holidays from Easter to September.

Above: The Victoria at Earl Soham brews its own beer and is well worth a visit.

Starting point(s): Earl Soham, A1120. Possible to start in Debenham and treat this section as a circular ride.

Parking: On-street in both Earl Soham and Debenham.

Public transport: Very limited. There is a relatively infrequent bus service between Ipswich (Cattle Market) and Debenham.

Distance: About 15 miles in total; circular route from Debenham about 4 miles.

Maps: Landranger 156 (Saxmundham & Aldeburgh); Pathfinders 985 (Debenham & Bacton) and 986 (Framlingham & Saxmundham).

Surfaces and gradients: Fairly easy ride. Small sections are on metalled lanes. Otherwise quite variable: some parts are

Above: This is what is meant by a 'green lane'! This is one of an excellent network of tracks in this part of High Suffolk.

grassy and potentially muddy, while others are old-established green lanes with compacted earth surfaces.

Roads and crossing points: Short section on the A1120 at Earl Soham, soon turning onto the lane to Bedfield. Section of almost 2 miles between Dog Corner and Ashfield Lodge on a quiet lane. Debenham circuit is almost entirely off-road.

National Cycle Network connections: Earl Soham is about 2 miles from Apsey Green, just outside Framlingham, along a quiet lane.

Refreshments: Victoria pub in Earl Soham; pubs, tea rooms and a renowned fish and chip shop in Debenham.

ROUTE INSTRUCTIONS
Starting from Earl Soham: go along the A1120 in the Yoxford direction and turn left along Badingham Road. After about ⅓ mile turn right, following an old bridleway sign. This takes you along a field headland; follow the hedge to the next lane. Turn left then right onto a bridleway at the next bend. Follow this until a T-junction, signed as a RUPP. Turn left. Continue to the next T-junction, turn right, signed to Bedfield and Tannington. Follow this bridleway; it may be muddy and rutted in places. Cross Dog Lane; the track onwards can be slightly overgrown. At the next T-junction turn left onto an excellent track. Turn right at Bedfield House, just in front of the church. Follow the track as far as the next lane, and turn left.

At Dog Corner (almost immediately) go right and continue along this lane (generally very quiet) to Bridge Cottage and Driver's Farm, on the Earl Soham to Kenton road. Turn left; this is a little busier. After

¼-mile turn right onto a signed bridleway just before Ashfield Lodge. It starts as a metalled track: don't divert off it, but go straight ahead until it turns into Waddlegoose Lane.

After about 1½ miles come to a Y-junction which effectively marks the start of the Debenham circuit. Waddlegoose Lane goes right. At the next junction, just under a mile, turn right, emerging onto Kenton Road: turn left and go along this quiet lane for a short distance. Immediately past the next cottages, turn right onto the signed bridleway and follow this into Debenham. It emerges in Water Lane; go straight ahead (right), but be warned that there is a ford ahead through the River Deben. In winter or spring it may be necessary to dismount and wheel bikes along the path on the right of the road. (Turning left instead of right from the bridleway bypasses the town centre; turn left at the end of this road, then right, then left to continue the circuit.)

From the centre of Debenham: turn left opposite the town sign, passing Bloomfield's works. Go over the river and turn right, and then left up a 'no through road' to Crows Hall. There is no significant traffic along this lane. After about ¾-mile turn left off the metalled road onto a signed bridleway. At the next junction go right (straight ahead) off the main track; the other track could be used to form a much shorter circuit. Follow this track for about 1½ miles back to the Y-junction mentioned earlier, and return to Earl Soham. Note that it is possible to shorten this by turning right at Ashfield Lodge, then left almost immediately at Clowes Corner, following Low Road back to Earl Soham. This road can be quite busy, especially where it joins the A1120.

Above: Debenham's town sign, reflecting the importance of the wool trade, and also the fact that the River Deben was navigable thus far.

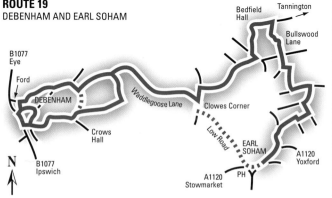

ROUTE 19
DEBENHAM AND EARL SOHAM

ALTON WATER

PLACES OF INTEREST ALONG THE ROUTE

Alton Water itself is a major water sports centre, as well as an important site for bird watching. East Bergholt, about 8 miles to the west, has strong connections with John Constable.

Above: Anglian Water has made an important contribution to leisure and fitness with the cycle trails and water sports facilities at Alton Water since it opened.

Starting point: Alton Water visitor centre.

Parking: Alton Water visitor centre.

Public transport: Minimal. Nearest railway stations are Manningtree and Ipswich, each about 7 miles away.

Cycle hire: Alton Cycle Hire, at the visitor centre (01473 328873 or 328268).

Distance: About 8 miles.

Maps: OS Landranger 169 (Ipswich & The Naze).

Surfaces and gradients: On the southwest side of the reservoir the path is in much better condition, having been recently renovated, and has a very good, hard and even surface. On the northwest it is less good and can be muddy; there are also some steep gradients this side. The Tattingstone bridge links the two sides at the western end.

Above: One end of the dam at Alton Water.

Roads and crossing points: Tattingstone bridge.

National Cycle Network connections: Ipswich is the closest point.

Refreshments: Café at the visitor centre.

There are pubs in Tattingstone and Holbrook; those in Stutton involve going onto the busy B1080.

ROUTE INSTRUCTIONS
Not necessary. Follow the signs from the visitor centre.

Above: Alton Water: ready for the off!

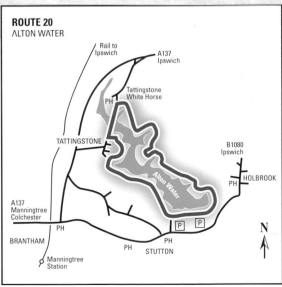

ROUTE 20
ΛLTON WATER

Rail to
Ipswich

A137
Ipswich

Tattingstone
White Horse

PH

TATTINGSTONE

B1080
Ipswich

PH HOLBROOK

Alton Water

A137
Manningtree
Colchester

PH

P P

BRANTHAM

PH

PH STUTTON

Manningtree
Station

N

IPSWICH

PLACES OF INTEREST ALONG THE ROUTE

Ipswich has many attractions; see also the 'Refreshments' section. Christchurch Mansion (01473 253246) dates from the 16th century and is set in fine parkland in the town centre. It contains much fine furniture, pottery and porcelain, and houses the most important collection outside London of paintings by Thomas Gainsborough and John Constable; not open Mondays. Ipswich Transport Museum (01473 715666) in Cobham Road is devoted to the town's history, and is housed in the old trolleybus depot. It opens daily during August, and Sundays from mid-April to October. Ipswich Museum (01473 213761) is in High Street and has collections of local interest.

Starting point(s): Ipswich rail station, Westerfield station, Derby Road station.

Parking: Park-and-ride at Pinebrook (near A12/A14 interchange); various sites in the town; parking is difficult in Ipswich. Don't try the railway station.

Public transport: Anglia and Great Eastern Railways services to Ipswich from London,

Below: Christchurch Mansion, in the heart of Ipswich, houses important art collections, and is surrounded by magnificent formal parkland.

Above: Ipswich also boasts some interesting modern architecture, such as the Willis Faber building, on the route from the railway station into the town centre.

Essex, Suffolk and Norfolk; Westerfield is on the Lowestoft and Felixstowe lines, and Derby Road on the Felixstowe line. Buses from all parts of Suffolk and north Essex.

Cycle hire: Bicycle Doctor & Hire, 18 Bartholomew Street (01473 259853); Alford Bros, 119-121 Hamilton Road, Felixstowe IP11 7BL, (01394 284719).

Maps: OS Landranger 169 (Ipswich & The Naze); Cycle Ipswich route map (from Tourist Information Centre, St Stephen's Lane (01473 258072); Sustrans Fakenham to Harwich, panel 4.

Surfaces and gradients: Mostly metalled. Ipswich has grown around the River Gipping, and whilst there are no steep gradients, it can be a steady pull up out of the valley.

Roads and crossing points: The centre of Ipswich is very poor for cycling and has almost no off-road cycle routes. Further out, particularly in Kesgrave and Martlesham to the east, and on the route out to Claydon in the northwest, matters are better. Kesgrave High School has the highest proportion of pupils cycling to school in Britain, about 60%.

National Cycle Network connections: The Colchester to Woodbridge route skirts the west of Ipswich.

Refreshments: Ipswich has all facilities. Note the availability of tours of the Tolly Cobbold Brewery (01473 231723 day, 01473 281508 evenings), and the Ipswich Parks, Dock and Brewery Circular Tour (usually by open-top bus, 0800 919390).

ROUTE 21
IPSWICH

To Bramford Lane and
Claydon via Old Norwich Road
Routes start about
1 mile from rail station

Wheel bike past
closed road

Tower
Ramparts
Bus Station

Traffic free

County
Hall

Butter Market
traffic free,
cycle one-way

Ipswich
Town FC

Country
Bus Station

To Kesgrave and
Martlesham via
Woodbridge Road
Cycle route starts
1/2 mile from station,
off-road about 2 miles
from station

Ranelagh
Road

River Gipping

Route starts
1/2 mile from station
To London Road
off-road cycle route to
Park & Ride and Copdock

Ipswich
Rail Station

To Wherstead Road and
Maidenhall Approach
Connects to Route 20

Many one-way streets

N

ROUTE INSTRUCTIONS

If you visit Ipswich by bike and wish to avoid traffic, your best bet is probably to park it at the station and take a bus into town. There are racks outside at the front of the car park, and lockers on the main platforms. 'Anglia Plus' rail tickets entitle the holder to a free direct bus journey from the station to any point within the Ipswich Borough boundary and back, and other local rail tickets can be bought with an add-on to 'Ipswich Buses' for only 20p extra (valid on Ipswich Buses and First Eastern Counties), both serving the station.

Otherwise, follow the cycle route map, but beware that Princes Street (opposite the station, going into town) is not a minor road, but that part of it is for buses only.

Left: Anglia Railways, in common with other train operators, is making increasing provision for cycle parking. This is the scene at Ipswich station, where there are more lockers on the main platform.

DUNWICH TO THORPENESS

PLACES OF INTEREST ALONG THE ROUTE

Dunwich is a village steeped in history; more details are given under Route 18. Dunwich Heath is a National Trust property (01728 648505) and noted for its wildlife. Much of Suffolk to the east of the A12 is known generally as 'the Sandlings' and historically the landscape has been heathland. The light sandy soil has been much cultivated for vegetables, and there is now considerable effort by conservationists, led by the Suffolk Wildlife Trust, to retain the remaining untouched areas for wildlife. The coast — which in many places is very unstable and liable to rapid erosion, as at Dunwich — has areas of estuary, mudflats and reedbeds, and is of major importance for bird life, especially waders. The Royal Society for the Protection of Birds established its reserve at Minsmere soon after World War 2, and the return of the avocet as a breeding species is one of its major achievements. It

is now working to increase the bittern population. The reserve is open daily except Tuesdays.

Leiston is nearby and was once the home of Richard Garrett's engineering works, builders of steam engines. Closed for many years, part has been incorporated into the Long Shop museum, giving a fascinating glimpse into the industrial past of Suffolk, as well as having displays of wartime memorabilia. It is open daily from April to October (01728 832189). At the other end of the technological spectrum is the Sizewell Visitor Centre. Nuclear Electric offers tours of the stations as well as nature trails; admission is free (01728 653890). Thorpeness is an eccentric Edwardian seaside resort and retains an air of quaint gentility. You can go boating on the Meare, tour the windmill or admire the House in the Clouds. This last is actually a water tower, and being also a private house is not open to the public.

Above: The House in the Clouds at Thorpeness, with the tail of the windmill. The house is really a water tank, although the lower part is a private residence.

Above: Heading north from Thorpeness towards Sizewell, with the power station in the distance.

Right: Thorpeness Windmill, open to the public at some times in the summer season.

Starting point(s): Dunwich beach car park; Dunwich Heath car park.

Parking: As above.

Public transport: Minimal to Dunwich. On weekdays there is a regular bus service to Thorpeness from Woodbridge and Ipswich. Nearest rail stations: Darsham (for Dunwich); Saxmundham (for Thorpeness), both served by Anglia Railways.

Cycle hire: Byways Bicycles, Priory Farm, Priory Lane, Darsham, Saxmundham IP17 3QD (01728 668764).

Distance: About 9 miles each way. Links with Route 18.

Maps: OS Landranger 156 (Saxmundham & Aldeburgh).

Surfaces and gradients: Surfaces are very variable. There are short sections of metalling, some forest tracks which may be muddy and some heathland tracks which can be sandy. There are no significant steep gradients, but east Suffolk's Sandlings are much more undulating than might be imagined.

Roads and crossing points: The start is along a road which can be surprisingly busy: Dunwich is a tourist honeypot. Similarly, the route uses parts of the access roads to Minsmere bird reserve, and although they are narrow lanes with frequent speed humps, care is needed. There is a short section along a road through Sizewell Belts, but this is much less busy than its size suggests: it was widened to accommodate construction traffic for Sizewell B power station.

National Cycle Network connections: The nearest approaches are at Snape Maltings, or at Green Farm, west of Darsham.

Refreshments: Dunwich has the Ship Inn, noted for its fish and chips and good beer. The Beach Café also serves very good fish and chips. There is a National Trust tea room at Dunwich Heath. The Eel's Foot at Eastbridge and the Vulcan Arms at Sizewell both serve good beer and food. Minsmere has a café and restaurant, while Thorpeness has cafés, pubs and tea shops.

ROUTE INSTRUCTIONS

Starting from the beach car park, go up the hill, past the Greyfriars ruins, and take the left turn (about ¾-mile) to Dunwich Heath. About ½-mile along this road take the signed bridleway to the right. This is a pleasant, easy track across open heath and woodland, but is sandy in places. Take care where the track crosses the Minsmere access road. Keep going until the track turns into the other Minsmere access near Eastbridge, and again take care.

Follow the metalled road through Eastbridge, past the Eel's Foot pub, taking a signed bridleway to the left about ½-mile after the pub. Follow it for about a mile, going left (actually straight ahead) onto the road to Sizewell. At the top of the hill bear left onto a bypassed loop of the road and soon take the track on the left.

After about ¼-mile turn right off the main track, following the fingerpost along the bridleway. Continue, crossing a grassy field (but keeping on the track), going right onto the much more prominent track which leads to the Sizewell road. The pavement on the opposite side is for shared cycle and pedestrian use: either go straight on for the Sizewell power stations and Vulcan Arms or turn right almost immediately (to Sizewell Hall) to stay on route.

At the end of the metalled road (this is a very quiet lane) go right (ignore the footpath sign). Continue for about ½-mile to a signed left turn uphill along a byway. This track is much less prominent. At the first choice, unsigned, bear left. The path becomes almost a green tunnel, and when it emerges, continue straight ahead onto the much more prominent one. Follow this downhill into Thorpeness. When you approach the metalled road, bear right and cross the road into 'The Sanctuary', signed as a byway, which will bring you out opposite the Meare.

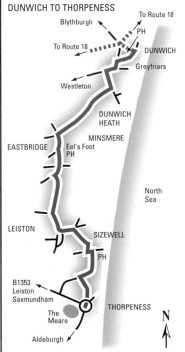

ROUTE 22
DUNWICH TO THORPENESS

To Route 18
Blythburgh
PH
To Route 18
DUNWICH
Greyfriars
Westleton
DUNWICH HEATH
MINSMERE
EASTBRIDGE   Eel's Foot PH
North Sea
LEISTON
SIZEWELL
PH
B1353
Leiston
Saxmundham
THORPENESS
The Meare
N
Aldeburgh

LOWESTOFT

PLACES OF INTEREST

Apart from having Britain's most easterly point (Ness Point) Lowestoft is a working port, with fishing still a significant activity. The offshore oil industry is serviced from here and the harbour is increasingly busy with commercial traffic. In addition, there is much development work in progress on a new marina in the outer harbour, with a section devoted to moorings for historic vessels, including the Mincarlo.

Lowestoft has much to offer visitors. The South Beach consistently wins Blue Flag awards and is a fine stretch of sand. There is much argument about whether cycling should be allowed on the sea front; at the time of writing it is not. The striking, modern East Point Pavilion offers tourist information and other facilities, while there are two piers. The town is bisected by Lake Lothing, which forms the inner harbour and is connected to the outer harbour by a narrow shipping channel spanned by a lifting bridge. When this goes up, traffic on the A12 grinds to a halt.

Pleasurewood Hills American Theme Park is at Corton, open mid-May to mid-September, and at certain other times. At the Sparrows Nest park at the northern end of the town are formal gardens, the Naval Museum, the Lowestoft Memorial Museum and a theatre. The Isca maritime museum in Caldecott Road, Oulton Broad, recently moved from Exeter and houses a fine collection of craft of all kinds. The East Anglian Transport Museum (01502 518459)

Above: There has been much redevelopment of Lowestoft's outer harbour in recent years, creating a marina and viewing area for historic vessels.

at Carlton Colville has interesting collections of buses and trams, the former occasionally being allowed out on the road: open weekends Easter to September and daily in the school summer holidays. The Tourist Information Centre in the East Point Pavilion has full details (01502 523000).

There are several nature reserves in the area, the most notable being at Carlton Marshes, in Burnt Hill Lane. In addition, Foxburrow Wood and Leathes Ham are also of interest, and all are maintained by the Suffolk Wildlife Trust (01502 564250).

Parking: Lowestoft railway station; East Point Pavilion; Gordon Road (multi-storey), Belvedere Road.

Public transport: Anglia Railways' train services from Ipswich and Norwich. There are also stations at Oulton Broad South (on the East Suffolk line from Ipswich) and Oulton Broad North, on the Norwich line. First Eastern Counties buses serve the town from Great Yarmouth, Norwich, Southwold, Beccles and most surrounding areas.

Cycle hire: Norfolk & Suffolk Cycle Centre, London Road South, Lowestoft (01502

585968); P. B. Cycles, Tower Mills, Southwold Road, Wrentham (01502 675516).

Maps: OS Landranger 134 (Norwich & The Broads); Pathfinder 925 (Lowestoft & Beccles North); Cycle Lowestoft route map (available from most Suffolk County Council libraries and local Tourist Information Centres).

Surfaces and gradients: No significant gradients. Surfaces are generally metalled.

Roads and crossing points: Many routes within Lowestoft are cycles lanes on roads,

Below: At Oulton Broad there is a sea lock which gives access between the Broads and the sea. When the road bridge was replaced a few years ago, the opportunity was taken to install new traffic-free cycling facilities.

Left: The start of the cycle path along the former railway line from Kirkley to Oulton Broad, reached from the Belvedere Road car park

some busy. There is an increasing number of off-road routes, including the Railpath along the former Lowestoft to Yarmouth railway line, now partly open.

National Cycle Network connections: Beccles (8 miles) is the nearest point at the moment.

Refreshments: Lowestoft has all facilities.

ROUTE INSTRUCTIONS

Consult the Lowestoft cycle map for full details of routes; however, treat it with care, as it is a little misleading in places. The main routes are:

1. From the railway station, go south and cross lifting bridge. It is possible to cycle over it, but it is the A12 and it may be easier to wheel bikes across (preferably without crossing the road). Either follow the signs or wheel right into Belvedere Road and then follow the cycle route sign left. This starts in a car park on the site of Kirkley goods station and picks up the line of the old railway. Follow the signs; it can take you to

Oulton Broad or Carlton Colville, the latter mostly off-road or on minor roads. If going to Oulton Broad, you will cross Colville Road by a mini-roundabout. It may be preferable to turn left and then right into Dell Road to avoid being routed onto the busy Victoria Road.

2. Bridge Road, bypassed when the new swing bridge was built, provides good, quiet cycle access; Caldecott Road can be reached without emerging onto the main A1117.

It is possible to reach the Railpath and Footpath 21 (through Normanston Park) via Denmark Road and Rotterdam Road (turn left out of the railway station), but they are very busy. It may be better to wheel bikes through London Road North (pedestrianised) and pick up the route at Milton Road, a little further north. Follow the signs.

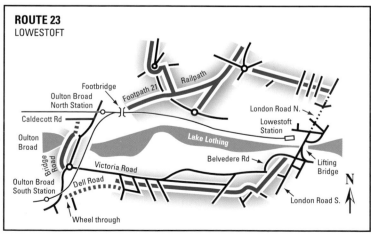

ROUTE 23
LOWESTOFT

Footbridge
Oulton Broad North Station
Caldecott Rd
Oulton Broad
Footpath 21
Railpath
London Road N.
Lowestoft Station
Lake Lothing
Bridge Road
Oulton Broad South Station
Victoria Road
Dell Road
Belvedere Rd
Lifting Bridge
London Road S.
Wheel through

N

FLITCH WAY — BRAINTREE TO GREAT DUNMOW

PLACES OF INTEREST ALONG THE ROUTE

Blake House Craft Centre (01376 320662) is at Blake End, just off the A120 near Rayne.

Above: Heading for Great Dunmow, having just come off the Flitch Way proper.

Starting point: Braintree railway station.

Parking: Braintree railway station, Rayne station.

Braintree District Museum (01376 325266) is housed in an old Victorian school in Manor Street and tells the story of the town up to the present day; the Working Silk Museum is 5min away (01376 553393). The Town Hall Centre, Tourist Information and Art Gallery are adjacent to the museum (01376 550066). A little further away is Cressing Temple, an impressive complex of medieval buildings open Sunday to Friday (01376 584903); nearest station is actually White Notley.

Public transport: Great Eastern Railway trains to Braintree. Bus services from most parts of Essex.

Cycle hire: Channels Mountain Bike Centre, Little Waltham (01245 441000).

Distance: Just under 9 miles one way.

Maps: OS Landranger 167 (Chelmsford & Harlow); Flitch Way leaflet from Essex County Council Ranger Service at Rayne station (01376 340262) or Country Parks Information (01277 261343).

Surfaces and gradients: No significant gradients on the route itself, but there are places where bridges have been removed and it is necessary to manhandle your bike up or down on and off the track. The surface is generally good — compacted ballast, firm and well drained.

Roads and crossing points: A120 near Rayne station; a diversion along minor roads crosses it by bridge. Minor road at

Felsted old station. The Flitch Way does not go into Great Dunmow itself, and access thence is on roads. Cycle access connecting with the western end of the Flitch Way is very poor indeed.

National Cycle Network connections: The projected Lea Valley to Harwich route passes through Chelmsford.

Refreshments: Braintree and Great Dunmow have all facilities. Pubs in Felsted and Little Dunmow, each about ¾-mile off the route, and in Rayne.

ROUTE INSTRUCTIONS
Leave Braintree station and turn left: access to the Flitch Way is clearly signed through the car park. Directions are largely unnecessary, since the route follows the former railway almost all the way. Two points:
1. To avoid crossing the A120 on the level, turn left at the old level crossing at Rayne station and go over the bridge (not down School Road). Continue for about ¼-mile to Mill Road and turn right. Follow this to the Flitch Way, joining it by turning right immediately before the bridge.

2. At the Great Dunmow end, the track goes over a byway close to the River Chelmer. Descend to this byway (access here is poor) and follow it to the main A130. Cross this to join Chelmsford Road into Great Dunmow.

Below: Mixed use on the Flitch Way near Great Dunmow.

ROUTE 24
FLITCH WAY- BRAINTREE TO GREAT DUNMOW

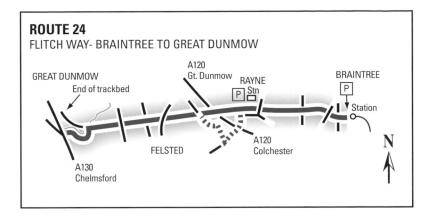

Above: Rayne station has been restored and refurbished by Essex County Council and is used as a base for their country park rangers. It also houses toilets and exhibitions, and provides information for users of the Flitch Way.

FLITCH WAY — GREAT DUNMOW TO TAKELEY

PLACES OF INTEREST ALONG THE ROUTE

Starting point: Easton Lodge station car park.

Parking: Easton Lodge car park; also Tilekiln Green, reached by turning left very shortly before the A120 crosses the M11; the old railway crosses by a bridge.

Public transport: Buses between Great

Hatfield Forest is a National Trust property, with a country park and nature trail. It is a national nature reserve (01279 871938). Stansted Airport is difficult to miss, with planes flying frequently over the western end of the route.

Dunmow and Bishop's Stortford and Stansted.

Distance: About 5 miles one way.

Maps: OS Landranger 167 (Chelmsford & Harlow); Flitch Way leaflet (from Essex County Council Ranger Service at Rayne

Below: Cycling connections between the halves of the Flitch Way are poor. The best place to park for access to the western end is at Easton Lodge Halt.

Above: The buildings at Easton Lodge Halt are in private ownership, and the Flitch Way diverts from the trackbed on the other side.

station (01376 340262) or Country Parks Information (01277 261343).

Surfaces and gradients: No significant gradients on the route itself, but there are places where bridges have been removed and it is necessary to manhandle your bike up or down on and off the track. The surface is generally very good — firm and well drained.

Roads and crossing points: Some bridges have been removed, necessitating crossing of lanes on the level. The Flitch Way does not go into Great Dunmow itself, and access thence is on roads. Cycle access connecting with the eastern end of the Flitch Way is very poor indeed. Don't try the official leaflet's suggestion of cycling along the A120.

National Cycle Network connections: The projected Harlow to Cambridge route passes through Bishop's Stortford.

Refreshments: Bishop's Stortford and Great Dunmow have all facilities. Shops and pubs in Takeley and Takeley Street. Hatfield Forest has a lakeside café.

ROUTE INSTRUCTIONS
The route westbound starts immediately to the north of the old level crossing at Easton Lodge, skirting the former platform. Follow the old trackbed. There is major structural failure on a bridge near Canfield End, with a signed diversion across a field. Take care where lorries access the local rubbish tip. Past Takeley station look out for access to Hatfield Forest. The end of the route is clearly signed at Tilekiln Green, but the track continues a further ¼-mile.

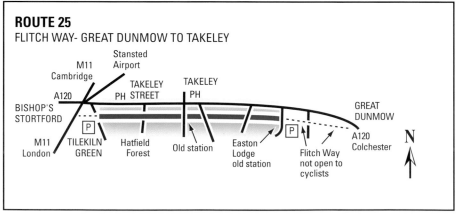

ROUTE 25
FLITCH WAY- GREAT DUNMOW TO TAKELEY

Stansted
Airport

M11
Cambridge

TAKELEY   TAKELEY
PH STREET   PH

A120

BISHOP'S
STORTFORD

GREAT
DUNMOW

A120
Colchester

M11   TILEKILN   Hatfield   Old station   Easton   Flitch Way
London   GREEN   Forest   Lodge   not open to
                                                old station   cyclists

N

Top: Takeley station is more or less derelict, although access to the village is possible from this point.

STEBBING AND BARDFIELD SALING

PLACES OF INTEREST ALONG THE ROUTE

Andrewsfield USAF Base was the first to be built in Britain during World War 2. The route covers a part of it, and light planes still fly from here. Bardfield Saling church has some fine examples of straw plaiting and some interesting graffiti. The squeeze-stile by the gate is unusual. Saling Hall Garden, Great Saling (01371 850243) is a 17th-century walled garden with a small park. Great Bardfield Cage is a 19th century village one-man lock-up; free admission! Great Bardfield cottage museum (01371 810838) is a 16th-century charity cottage with a collection including rural crafts; free admission.

Above: This excellent track effectively bypasses Stebbing.

Starting point: Stebbing.

Parking: Stebbing.

Public transport: Very limited bus services to Stebbing. The route could be accessed from the Flitch Way (see Route 24), but this involves crossing the A120.

Cycle hire: Channels Mountain Bike Centre, Little Waltham (01245 441000).

Distance: About 9 miles.

Maps: OS Landranger 167 (Chelmsford & Harlow); Pathfinder 1075 (Great Dunmow &

Braintree); Essex County Council 'Ways through Essex' leaflet 'Bardfield Saling'.

Surfaces and gradients: A fairly easy ride. Surfaces are generally good, although there are a few potentially muddy tracks. Some gentle gradients.

Roads and crossing points: A few short sections are on minor lanes.

National Cycle Network connections: The projected Lea Valley to Harwich route passes through Chelmsford.

Refreshments: King's Head pub in Stebbing, and village shop; the White Hart at Great Saling is about a mile off the route. Pubs and shops in Great Bardfield.

ROUTE INSTRUCTIONS

On-street parking is possible in Stebbing village. Go south along the main street, turn left past the church and left into Whitehouse Road (leading into Lubberhedges Lane), this last about half a mile from the start. Follow this lane for about a mile. Go right at the public

bridleway sign, through the gate to Gatehouse Farm, heeding the sign which asks you to 'Please Drive Slowly — Ducks on Driveway'. The track becomes rough and grassy for a short distance; emerge by battery chicken houses (phew!) on to a concrete track. There is a choice at this point:

1. Either go right, then left on to the road (an old runway) and pass the airstrip on your right. At the end of the 'runway' take an acute left turn, quite unmarked — look out for old concrete fenceposts marking the track. Follow this. Emerge at a much better track signed as a byway and go right.

2. Or go left and take the next right, clearly signed. At the next junction go left, rejoining the route above. This way is easier.

Continue to Gentleman's Farm in Bardfield Saling. (For the pub at Great Saling, turn right when you get to the road, then left, left and right. A footpath can cut off the last corner, but note its status.) Go left towards the village, as far as St Peter & St Paul's church; Arundel House is

opposite. Go right on to the unsigned track just past the house. Continue to the metalled lane and turn left; left again at the next T-junction, going into the village. The road curves left; take the right turn signed as a cart track.

At the end of the metalling turn right and follow the track called Long Green. At the next junction you can take the right turn for Great Bardfield. Straight ahead goes to Bushett Farm; take the left turn on to a good track across the field. Bear left at the next junction, and then left on to a quiet lane.

About a mile further turn left on to a public byway. At the first junction (under ¼-mile) go left, then right almost at once. Emerge back on to the lane and turn right, then left after 100yd on to a byway. Follow this in a more or less southwesterly direction back to Stebbing. At the end of the track, either go left to come out at the church end of the village, or go right then left to get back quickly to the main street.

Above: St Peter & St Paul's church at Bardfield Saling.

Opposite page: Andrewsfield USAF base played an important role in World War 2, and still sees use by light aircraft.

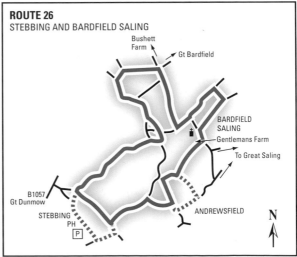

ROUTE 26
STEBBING AND BARDFIELD SALING

Bushett Farm · Gt Bardfield · BARDFIELD SALING · Gentlemans Farm · To Great Saling · B1057 Gt Dunmow · STEBBING PH · ANDREWSFIELD · N

ROUTE 27

THE BELCHAMPS

PLACES OF INTEREST ALONG THE ROUTE

Sudbury is a pleasant market town, now bypassed and with much pedestrianisation in the centre. Long Melford, about three miles to the north is a major centre for the antiques trade and featured in the TV series Lovejoy. Melford Hall (01787 880286) and Kentwell Hall (01787 310207) are well-known stately homes, the latter especially noted for its historic re-enactments. Sudbury Tourist Information Centre is in Market Hill (01787 881320).

Cavendish and Clare are both historic and picturesque towns. Cavendish has a vineyard (01787 280221), while the Clare Castle Country Park (01787 277491) offers a range of attractions. Look out for Pentlow Tower on Pentlow Hill. It is a folly some 90ft tall, eight-sided and built of brick. Whilst not on the route itself, it should be visible, although please bear in mind that it is on private property.

Above: The Valley Walk starts near Sudbury railway station and follows the trackbed of the former line towards Long Melford, although stopping short of the latter. This bridge takes it over the River Stour.

Starting point: Sudbury station. It would also be possible to start at Clare or Cavendish, both just off the route.

Parking: Local authority car park at Sudbury Leisure Centre, next to the station. Clare or Cavendish town centres; the Half Moon at Belchamp St Paul.

Public transport: Great Eastern Railway from Mark's Tey to Sudbury station; bus service (about two-hourly) between Sudbury, Long Melford, Cavendish, Clare and Haverhill.

Cycle hire: Suffolk Cycle Centre, Sudbury bus station (01787 310940); Cycles Store, Sudbury (01787 881810).

Distance: About 18 miles in total. The route is mostly circular, with a common section of about 3 miles each way, out and back from the station.

Maps: OS Landranger 155 (Bury St Edmunds & Sudbury).

Above: It is worth diverting into Clare, which has a range of facilities and much of architectural interest. This is a superb example of pargetting (relief plasterwork) on a house by the church.

Surfaces and gradients: Overall, a very challenging ride. There are some steep gradients and it is a long pull up out of the Stour Valley from Clare. Surfaces can be very poor, including muddy or stony. In addition, some parts, although designated and signed as bridleways or byways, are rather overgrown. On the other hand, the section of former railway known as 'Valley Walk' out of Sudbury is very easy.

Roads and crossing points: There are some sections on roads (almost all very quiet), but it may be felt desirable to make the ride an 'out and back' from Sudbury via Belchamp St Paul to minimise them. There is a short stretch on the B1064 near Cavendish.

National Cycle Network connections: Colchester and Hadleigh are on the Harwich-Hull route.

Refreshments: Sudbury and Clare have all facilities. Cavendish is smaller, but has pubs. The Half Moon at Belchamp St Paul has excellent real ale and food.

ROUTE INSTRUCTIONS

1. On leaving Sudbury station, the Leisure Centre is immediately ahead. Follow signs to 'main entrance', turning left immediately past the building. Keeping on paved path and the leisure centre on the left, look out for the 'Valley Walk' sign.

2. After about two miles a track crosses diagonally and is waymarked 'Stour Valley Path' — turn left. Follow field headlands for about a mile and emerge at a new road bridge. Turn right on to the road, and left almost immediately. BEWARE: although minor, the road can be busy.

3. After ¾-mile, take the third turn on the right. This is a quiet minor road and after about ½-mile turns sharp right. This is where the route rejoins on return to Sudbury. However, go straight ahead along the signed bridleway.

4. At the end of this track (about ½-mile) continue straight ahead.

5. BEWARE (about ¼-mile) of a narrow bridge, which is easy not to see. Bear left soon afterwards.

6. The track goes quite sharply uphill for about ¼-mile; at the junction turn very sharp right. This is difficult because of the slope and difference in levels. This track is also a green lane but very overgrown; it is just about passable. There are reassuring waymarks en route!

7. Emerge on to a field edge; the route is waymarked, but almost disappears. It follows the field edge, with the boundary on the left, and the next ¼-mile is difficult. Continue to the next waymark and on to a much better track on the headland.

Above: A pleasant section of
bridleway near Bower Hall,
between Cavendish and Clare.

ROUTE 27
THE BELCHAMPS

8. Continue to the
farmhouse, keeping straight
ahead and picking up the
metalled road. Follow it into
Belchamp St Paul and the
Half Moon pub.
9. Continue along the road
for about 300yd and take the
marked bridleway on the
right. Turn left on to the
minor road.
10. After about ¾-mile look
for a turning on the left to Knowl Green,
but go right on to the clearly-signed 'Public
Byway'. This drops steadily down the valley
side towards Clare.
11. At the end turn left on to the road if you
wish to get into Clare. The route turns
right, however, and forks left after about
¼-mile on to a good track which is a
bridleway.
12. After a further ⅛-mile turn right (this
can be difficult to see, but is waymarked)
and go uphill. Follow this track for about
two miles past Bower Hall: it turns left just
before the hall on to a better track. It
emerges at Pentlow; continue straight

ahead for about ½-mile along this busy road.
13. Take the marked 'Public Byway' uphill
for about ¾-mile.
14. At the metalled road turn left, then right
at Buntings Farm, keeping to the metalled
road. After about ¼-mile there is a turning
to Foxearth; take this if you wish to go to
Long Melford. (Go along the B1064 a short
way and push your bike up the footpath to
the hall: there is then a good metalled track
down to Liston, and a very quiet lane into
Melford.)
15. On the other hand, if you continue along
the road through Temple End it brings you
back to the divergence of the ways (see 3),
and takes you back to Sudbury.

PLESHEY

PLACES OF INTEREST ALONG THE ROUTE

Pleshey Castle is open by prior appointment only (01245 360239). The castle itself has gone, but the Norman earthworks still ring the village. In William Shakespeare's Richard II, the Duchess of Gloucester urges Edmund York:

'With all good speed at Plashy visit me.
Alack, and what shall good old York there see
But empty lodgings and unfurnished walls
Unpeopled offices, untrodden stones?'

Even then, the castle was evidently in a bad way.

Hylands Park at Writtle, just to the southwest of Chelmsford, includes Victorian formal gardens, lakes and woods; free admission. Leez Priory at Hartford End is a 16th-century Tudor mansion with 13th-century priory ruins, parkland, lakes and walled gardens; essential to phone first (01245 362555).

Above: Pleshey is a pleasant, quiet village in the Essex countryside, and still has two pubs.

Starting point(s): Gravel lay-by about ¼-mile north of Fanner's Green on the road to Great Waltham (OS grid ref TL 683126); Pleshey village; Great Waltham.

Parking: At the starting points.

Public transport: Great Eastern and Anglia train services to Chelmsford station (about 4 miles); bus services from all parts of Essex to the adjacent bus station; services

to Braintree and Dunmow pass about 2 miles away along the B1008. Limited services to Great Waltham, about ½-mile off the route.

Cycle hire: Channels Mountain Bike Centre, Little Waltham (01245 441000).

Distance: About 9 miles, circular.

Maps: OS Landranger 167 (Chelmsford &

Harlow); Pathfinder 1098 (Great and Little Waltham).

Surfaces and gradients: A fairly easy ride. Most of the off-road sections are on old green lanes, many wooded, others more open. Some surfaces may sometimes be muddy, although generally good. No significant gradients.

Roads and crossing points: There is a short section on the road between Fanner's Green and Great Waltham which can be moderately busy, as can the lanes crossed north of High Houses and west of Pleshey village; otherwise the sections of lane are extremely quiet.

National Cycle Network connections: The main east coast route (1) runs via Chelmsford, from the Lea Valley to Maldon, Colchester and Harwich. Route 13 has a spur from Basildon to Chelmsford.

Refreshments:
Pleshey has two pubs: the White Horse (noted for its food) and the Leather Bottle, also serving food and excellent beer.

ROUTE INSTRUCTIONS
Starting near Fanner's Green, there is a signed bridleway which marks the end of the route. Go along the road northward, taking the first turn left along Humphreys Farm Lane, signed to Pleshey, Mashbury and the Easters. Turn right at the end of this lane and go through High Houses, then left (straight ahead) into Bury Lane, the main road going right to Great Waltham. (If starting there, this road starts opposite the church and goes in a general westerly direction.) A short distance out of the village there is a ford. Continue to the T-junction and cross (take care) on to the signed byway. Now a very pleasant green lane, this was once the main Dunmow to Chelmsford Road.

Do not be alarmed at the sound of traffic: the route approaches the A130 but does not quite get there. Turn left on approaching it, go left past Ringtail Green, and right at Rolphy Green, signed to Park Farm. After a

Below: A fine floral display in Pleshey.

concrete surface, shortly turning right on to a signed bridleway. Go along a headland for a short distance. Follow this series of pleasant green lanes (there is a short stretch where both hedges have been removed) into Chignall Smealy. Continue straight ahead, on the lane for about ¼-mile, and then left to Beadles Hall. Past this the lane turns back into a bridleway. Follow this (the first left bridleway offers a route back to Pleshey, all off-road) straight ahead until a cottage and a much larger track. The left route offers yet another way to Pleshey; continue straight ahead, returning to the start after a further ½-mile.

Left: South of Pleshey the bridleway crosses a field headland.

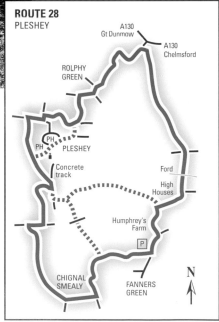

ROUTE 28
PLESHEY

A130
Gt Dunmow

A130
Chelmsford

ROLPHY
GREEN

PH
PH   PLESHEY

Concrete
track

Ford

High
Houses

Humphrey's
Farm

P

CHIGNAL
SMEALY

FANNERS
GREEN

N

further ¼-mile take the signed bridleway on the left. The total distance on this lane section is slightly over a mile. Follow this a short way to a T-junction and go right. Almost at once there is another junction: continue straight ahead. (Taking the bridleway to the left will bring you out in Pleshey village rather sooner.)

Emerge on to the metalled lane and go left, then right almost immediately. Take the bridleway on the left (just under ¼-mile), and follow it to the next road. Cross this to continue on the route. (Turn left to go into Pleshey.)

Follow this track until it runs on to a

ROUTE 29

NEWPORT CIRCULAR

PLACES OF INTEREST ALONG THE ROUTE

Mole Hall Wildlife Park and Butterfly Pavilion is on the route, near Widdington, and houses flamingos, llamas, wallabies and chimpanzees, as well as otters and a range of domestic animals. Thaxted is a town dating back at least 900 years and has retained the features of many of the periods of its history. The church spire is a major landmark, and there are numerous old timber-framed buildings. There are many other attractions including John Webb's windmill (open weekend afternoons Easter to September, 01371 831153), the Local History Museum, and the Guildhall, open Sundays and Bank Holiday Mondays Easter to September.

Above: A short distance out of Newport the track passes a farm.

Starting point: Newport railway station.

Parking: Newport station.

Public transport: West Anglia Great Northern train services to Newport.

Cycle hire: Geoff's Bike Hire, 65 Devonshire Road, Cambridge (01223 365629); Cambridge Recycles, On the Roundabout, Newnham Road, Cambridge CB3 9EN (01223 506035); H. Drake, 56-60 Hills Road (01223 363468); Roses Cycles, 173 High Street, Chesterton (01223 356162/564607); Cycle King, 195 Mill Road, Cambridge (01223 212222).

Distance: About 16 miles, but various shorter options are available.

Maps: OS Landranger 167 (Chelmsford & Harlow).

Surfaces and gradients: The overall route is challenging. Surfaces are variable. There are sections along field headlands, most of

Left: Go whichever way you like! The blue bridleway signs also show that cycling is permitted; near Rook End.

ROUTE INSTRUCTIONS

Start from the London-bound platform at Newport station, where there is a gate into a lane; turn right. (If arriving from London, either cross the footbridge or go right at the end of the station approach, right over the railway bridge and right again, which will bring you out on to the same lane.) At the end of this lane, bear left at the sign, up an overgrown track. This emerges on to a field headland, which is much better. Continue to the lane and go straight ahead, turning right (straight ahead) after a very short distance (signed as a byway).

Follow this track. You will pass a wood on your left, after which an insignificant-looking and unsigned path curves left through the hedge — this is the byway. There is a black barn ahead and away to the right at this point. Follow the track, emerging on to a metalled lane by cottages; turn left.

After about ½-mile turn right up a signed byway. Follow this to a T-junction (this marks the start of the circular section) and go left. Follow this track to Hamperden End, turning left on to the larger lane. (Note that where the track becomes a metalled lane, more or less in the farmyard, there is a signed byway on the right. This is muddy, but can be used to make a short cut to Amberden Hall and Mole Hall — see later.) After about ¼-mile, turn right along a signed byway to Richmonds in the Wood. Follow this, turning right into the next lane. Follow the bridleway from Loves Farm in a southerly direction — it is clearly signed.

which are firm and grassy. Others use tracks, which may be stony; there are also parts which use metalled lanes, the majority of these being dead-ends. There are some steep gradients, mostly for fairly short sections, but care is needed.

Roads and crossing points: There are a few crossings of minor roads, plus a section of about a mile approaching Tingates, and a slightly longer distance between Suckstead Green and Sibleys. The B1051 is crossed twice.

National Cycle Network connections: The Lea Valley to Harwich section passes through Harlow and Chelmsford. If the proposed Harlow to Cambridge route is constructed, it will pass near or through Newport.

Refreshments: Newport has all facilities. Mole Hall Wildlife Park has refreshments and toilets. Thaxted is about two miles off the route and has all facilities.

Above: Crossing a field headland and descending into the valley near Rook End.

ROUTE 29
NEWPORT CIRCULAR

NEWPORT

Newport station

Rail to London

Mole Hall

HAMPERDEN END

CARE!

B1051 Thaxted

N

B1051 Bishop's Stortford

PH

Duton Hill

Emerge at a major track (beware — there may be heavy lorries on it) and go right. Pull up the hill about ¼-mile and turn left off the track at the top of the slope (this is not at all clear). You should come to the start of a green lane, with trees either side. This lane goes steeply downhill and has a poor surface in places.

At the bottom, cross the B1051 (take care) and take the lane towards Monk Street. This is narrow and will have some traffic — it is easily the busiest part of the route. Turn left at the crossroads and follow the lane for nearly a mile, turning right to Tilty Hill Farm. Bear right there, following the byway. Continue to the B1051 and cross it. Follow the minor lane for about 1¾ miles to Sibleys. Cross the road on to the excellent bridleway.

Emerge near Amberden Hall: turn left at the T-junction (the signed right turn will take you back to Hamperden End, as noted above). Follow the lane past Mole Hall Wildlife Park and turn right just past it. Follow the bridleway signs and come out at the junction mentioned above as marking the start of the circular section. Retrace the route back to Newport station.

COLCHESTER AND WIVENHOE

PLACES OF INTEREST ALONG THE ROUTE

Wivenhoe is a busy small town, although the name is probably more associated these days with Wivenhoe Park, home of the University of Essex. This is easily accessible and clearly signed from the cycle path, and also houses the Lakeside Theatre which presents a very wide range of material. Prices vary: call 01206 873261. Colchester prides itself on being 'Britain's oldest recorded town' and offers a wealth of attractions for all types of visitor. The Castle Museum offers trips through British history from Boudicca's time, and opens Mondays to Saturdays all year, and Sunday afternoons from March to November; there is an admission charge. St Botolph's Priory

was the first Augustinian priory in England and dates from the 12th century; admission is free. On the other hand, Colchester Leisure World in Cowdray Avenue (on the route detailed below) offers a very wide range of activities including leisure and fitness pools, squash courts, an activity hall, sports pitches and the Aquasprings sauna and spa experience. Admission varies with the activity undertaken.

Colchester also boasts a very fine regional shopping centre, with all the main stores represented. Now that the cycle route goes right through the centre, it has become much more accessible to those interested in sustainable transport. The Tourist Information Centre is at 1 Queen Street (01206 282920).

Above: The Wivenhoe Trail is sandwiched between the River Colne and the railway to Clacton for all of its route. This yacht has just passed Hythe Quay.

Starting point: Wivenhoe station. Any point could be used to pick up the Harwich-Hull route.

Parking: Wivenhoe station.

Public transport: Great Eastern train services to Wivenhoe or Hythe. Wivenhoe is well served by bus services. Colchester has two rail stations (Town and North, although the latter name is no longer used), the latter having both Anglia and Great Eastern services from London, Norfolk and Suffolk. There is a dense network of urban bus services, as well as those from surrounding areas.

Cycle hire: R&A Cycles, The Spinning Wheel, 16 Barfield Road, Mersea Island CO5 8QT (01206 384013); Colchester Cycle Stores, 50 St Johns Street (01206 563890); Pedal Partners, 12 East Street, Tollesbury (01621 869974).

Distance: Wivenhoe to Colchester is about 2½ miles; Colchester itself has a significant and growing amount of off-road and segregated provision.

Maps: OS Landranger 168 (Colchester & The Blackwater area); Sustrans Fakenham to Harwich, panel 5.

Surfaces and gradients: No significant gradients. Surfaces are mostly very good indeed, either metalled or consolidated aggregate.

Roads and crossing points: From Wivenhoe the route becomes a shared-use path and has a light-controlled crossing over the A134; Hawkins Road is busy but has a shared-use non-segregated pavement (but watch for parking on it). East Hill is also crossed with traffic lights.

National Cycle Network connections: All part of the National Cycle Network, except the connection to Colchester North station.

Refreshments: Wivenhoe has all facilities. There is a kiosk in the taxi office at Wivenhoe station. Colchester is a major regional centre and has all facilities.

Below: This gate marks the start of the newest section of route in Colchester, between Spurgeon Street and East Hill. Hythe station is nearby.

Above: Healthy exercise on the Wivenhoe Trail.

ROUTE INSTRUCTIONS

If arriving by train from the Colchester direction and you do not wish to carry your bike over the footbridge, there is another nearby exit. It involves a few steps up, then follows a track parallel to the railway. Turn right into a private road (there is a right of way) and come out by the rail bridge. Cross this and go back down towards the station; beware of traffic, including buses. Go through the station car park to get to the start of the trail which is well signed.

After about 1½ miles there is a right turn, clearly signed, to the University of Essex. Continue along by the river, reaching Colchester docks on the opposite bank and emerging on to the main road. Cross the road at the traffic lights and go right.

Turn left at the roundabout into Hawkins Road and cross the road (take care). The opposite pavement is signed for shared pedestrian/cycle use. Turn left at the end of Hawkins Road (right takes you to Hythe station), go over the old bridge, turning right at the end on to a short section of segregated path and into Haddon Park, a new road. Quickly turn right between a house and some three-storey flats and pick up the new cycle path by the river. (NOTE: there may be more path under construction to simplify this.)

Follow this path across waste ground,

keeping an eye open for the characteristic Sustrans Millennium Marker, go under the railway line and through allotments. Emerge via a new access point at the bottom of the very busy East Hill, which is crossed by traffic lights. Continue through pleasant parkland to the gates of Lower Castle Park: cycling is not permitted here, but clear signs give directions to destinations such as the town centre. Turn right over the bridge to continue on the route. Bear left and then sharp left on to the road, and then right at the barrier (a very short distance). Go past the SuperBowl and Leisure Centre, and right on to the main road, where there are segregated off-road cycle paths.

Cross the road at the traffic lights and either turn left for the North station and Ipswich Road or right to stay on NCN Route 1 (see Sustrans Fakenham to Harwich, panel 5). For the station, follow the path to the next roundabout, where it ends. Access to the station by cycle is poor, with green cycle lanes on the main carriageway. The opportunity was not taken to provide segregated access when the main rail bridge was rebuilt recently, which was a big disappointment.

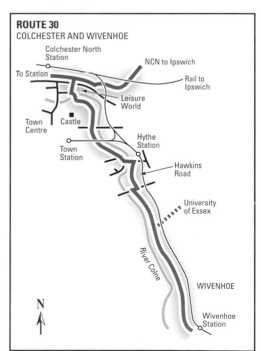

ROUTE 30
COLCHESTER AND WIVENHOE

Cambridgeshire County Council:
Environment and Transport, Castle Court, Shire Hall, Castle Hill, Cambridge CB3 0AP (Tel: 01223 717751; publications: 01223 717445)

Essex County Council:
Planning Department, County Hall, Chelmsford CM1 1LF (Tel: 01245 437647)

Norfolk County Council:
The Cycling Officer, County Hall, Norwich NR1 2SG (Tel: 01603 222230)

Suffolk County Council:
Planning and Transportation, St Edmund House, County Hall, Ipswich IP4 1LZ (Tel: 01473 583202).

Suffolk Connexions:
(for Suffolk publications) 36-38 St Helen's Street, Ipswich IP4 2JZ, (Tel: 01473 583000)

Bus Information Lines:
Cambridgeshire: 01223 717740
Essex: 0345 000333
Norfolk: 0500 626116
Suffolk: 0645 583358

National Rail Enquiry Service
Tel: 0345 484950

Anglia Railways:
Ipswich Station, Burrell Road, Ipswich IP2 8AL

Great Eastern Railway: Colchester Station, North Station Road, Colchester CO1 1XD

West Anglia Great Northern Railway: Station Road, Cambridge CB1 2JW

Central Trains: PO Box 4323, Stanier House, 10 Holliday Street, Birmingham B1 1TH

Right: A Sustrans Millennium Marker on the newest section of route in Colchester.

Sustrans:
35 King Street, Bristol BS1 4DZ (Tel: 0117 926 8893)
East of England office: 33a Westgate, Peterborough PE1 1PZ (Tel: 01733 319981)

Cyclists' Touring Club:
Cotterell House, 69 Meadrow, Godalming, Surrey GU7 3HS (Tel: 01483 417217)

Environmental Transport Association:
10 Church Street, Weybridge, Surrey KT13 8RS (Tel: 01932 828882)

Transport 2000:
Walkden House, 10 Melton Street, London NW1 2EJ (Tel: 0171 388 8386)

Forest Enterprise:
Tangham, Rendlesham Forest, Woodbridge, Suffolk IP12 3NF (Tel: 01394 450164)
Santon Downham, Brandon, Suffolk IP27 0TJ (Thetford Forest) (Tel: 01842 810271)

Anglian Water:
Alton Water Visitor Centre: (Tel: 01473 328628; general enquiries: 01572 653026)

Broads Authority:
18 Colegate, Norwich (Tel: 01603 610734)

As has been mentioned elsewhere, there are few opportunities for rides which are completely traffic-free. Those mentioned below can be followed with the aid of the appropriate Ordnance Survey maps, or using leaflets, usually produced by local authorities.

Cambridgeshire
'Cycling in the Fens': a pack of three leaflets, each detailing three routes around Ely, March and Wisbech. Cambs. County Council, £1.50 per pack

Cycling in the Ouse Valley: a pack of four leaflets describing routes around Huntingdon, St Ives and St Neots, plus three 'waterside routes'. Cambs County Council, £1.50

Cycling around Cambridge: a series of routes around the Cambridge greenbelt area, but mostly along lanes. Cambs County Council, £1.50

The Woodman's Way: a circular route of about 6½ miles from Wimblington, near March. It incorporates part of the old railway line between March and St Ives. Cambs County Council, 40p

Below: The Flitch Way follows the former railway from Braintree to Great Dunmow and Bishop's Stortford. Access for cyclists at the Dunmow end is via this track and a climb up just past the bridge.

The Bishop's Way: a circular route of about nine miles from Ely. Cambs County Council, 40p

Essex
Summer Country Rides, a series of six routes around The Belchamps, Pleshey, Bardfield Saling, Takeley, Clavering (west of Newport) and Basildon. The first three appear in modified form in this book. Essex County Council, £2.00

Witham River Route: off-road through the town centre. Essex County Council, free Ongar, Matching and the Lavers, a circular route on lanes, with access from Harlow Mill station. Essex County Council, free

A route is being developed along the course of the old railway between Witham and Maldon; contact the County Council for details

Directory of Walks and Rides: catalogue of available publications from Essex County Council, free

Below: Essex County Council rights of way signs are typically of this precast concrete type; this example is near Stebbing.

Norfolk

Peddars Way and North Norfolk Coast Path, Countryside Commission, free (from Norfolk County Council)

Norfolk Coast Cycleway:

Norfolk Coast by Bike. The route is the same as the National Cycle Network through the county, but the leaflet gives much additional information about accommodation, cycle hire and public transport. From Norfolk County Councils, district councils and Tourist Information Centres, £2.00

Cycling in the Mid-Wensum Valley:

routes connecting the Marriott's Way with Dereham and North Elmham; mostly on lanes but some off-road sections. Norfolk County Council, 20p. A further leaflet covers routes in the Fakenham area

The paths along the banks of the Old Bedford river and the Hundred Foot Drain south from Downham Market have bridleway status as far as the border with Cambridgeshire. This is also true of the Little Ouse river from Denver Sluice to Brandon and Santon Downham

Suffolk

Suffolk Coastal Cycle Route, a leaflet detailing this 75-mile circular ride, mostly along lanes, and with much now incorporated into the National Cycle Network. It connects the Suffolk forest

Below: The Brandon Country Park loop is the quieter of the two loops, and there is much more likelihood of seeing the abundant wildlife on this section in Thetford Forest.

rides in this book, and gives much information about accommodation, cycle hire and places of interest. Suffolk Connexions, 75p

Cycling in Suffolk, a suggested route around the entire county; details as above, 30p

Cycling around the Shotley Peninsula, a series of routes through a little-known part of the county; Suffolk Connexions, £1.00

Cycle Bury St Edmunds, a route map for the town; much off-road provision. Suffolk Connexions, free

Walks and Rides in Suffolk: a Directory, detailing all the available publications for the county; Suffolk Connexions, £1.00

Above: Belchamp St Paul church at Church Street, about a mile from the village, as seen from the bridleway.

Left: Fye Bridge, Norwich. This is an area for interesting shops and pubs.

Opposite page: Peterborough Cathedral west front, easily reached by bike from the station.